Writing
Fundamentals for the Middle-School Classroom

BY

CINDY BARDEN

CONSULTANT: SARAH M. ANDERSON

COPYRIGHT © 2010 Mark Twain Media, Inc.

ISBN 978-1-58037-556-6

Printing No. CD-404131

Mark Twain Media, Inc., Publishers
Distributed by Carson-Dellosa Publishing LLC

Visit us at www.carsondellosa.com

HPS   221292

Table of Contents

Introduction

As we move through the 21st century, written communication becomes increasingly important, yet it receives less and less attention in the classroom. With limited classroom time and resources, many teachers focus on content subjects (such as math and science) that can be measured through high-stakes standardized testing. While it is important for students to be knowledgeable in these content subjects, many teachers miss the opportunity to provide instruction on how to read and write about these subjects—and thereby miss the chance to teach students how to write in different formats for different purposes.

Writing is not just a tool with which to measure what a student already knows, such as a short answer essay on a history test. Writing is a learning process in itself. Students who can express themselves through writing will not only excel in school, but be prepared for life beyond primary education.

Research has shown that teachers can help students become better writers by differentiating writing instruction to fit a wide variety of writing needs and letting students develop a vested interest in writing by allowing them to choose their own topics. *Writing: Fundamentals for the Middle-School Classroom* helps students embrace writing by providing teachers with open-ended lessons in the five most common types of middle-school writing: personal writing, descriptive writing, short stories, poetry, and reports. Each chapter is arranged from easiest to most challenging, allowing teachers to let students write at their own level. The chapters are organized similarly, starting with personal writing and ending with the formal conventions of six different report styles. The lessons can be used together in order, as individual assignments, or as activities that supplement a pre-existing curriculum.

Writing: Fundamentals for the Middle-School Classroom supports students' continued development of comprehension strategies by engaging personal experiences to communicate with a variety of readers. Encourage students to write every day, to try different things, and most of all, to have fun!

NCTE Standards

Writing: Fundamentals for the Middle-School Classroom supports the following standards:

Standard 1: Students read a wide range of print and non-print texts to build an understanding of text, of themselves, and of the cultures of the United States and the world; to acquire new information; to respond to the needs and demands of society and the workplace; and for personal fulfillment. Among these texts are fiction and nonfiction, classic and contemporary works.

Standard 3: Students apply a wide range of strategies to comprehend, interpret, evaluate, and appreciate texts. They draw on their prior experiences, their interactions with other readers and writers, their knowledge of word meaning and of other texts, their word identification strategies, and their understanding of textual features (e.g., sound-letter correspondence, sentence structure, context, graphics).

Standard 4: Students adjust their use of spoken, written, and visual language (e.g., conventions, style, vocabulary) to communicate effectively with a variety of audiences and for different purposes

Standard 5: Students employ a wide range of strategies as they write and use different writing process elements appropriately to communicate with different audiences for a variety of purposes.

Standard 6: Students apply knowledge of language structure, language conventions (e.g., spelling and punctuation), media techniques, figurative language, and genre to create, critique, and discuss print and non-print texts.

Standard 7: Students conduct research on issues and interests by generating ideas and questions, and by posing problems. They gather, evaluate, and synthesize data from a variety of sources (e.g., print and non-print texts, artifacts, people) to communicate their discoveries in ways that suit their purpose and audience.

Standard 8: Students use a variety of technological and information resources (e.g., libraries, databases, computer networks, video) to gather and synthesize information and to create and communicate knowledge.

Standard 11: Students participate as knowledgeable, reflective, creative, and critical members of a variety of literacy communities.

Standard 12: Students use spoken, written, and visual language to accomplish their own purposes (e.g. for learning, enjoyment, persuasion, and the exchange of information).

National Council of Teachers of English/International Reading Association (1998). *NCTE/IRA Standards for the English Language Arts.* Urbana, IL. 5 Oct. 2009. <www.ncte.org/standards>

Name: _____ Date: _____

Many Types of Personal Writing

➡ People write letters to friends and relatives to invite people to events, to thank them for gifts or favors, and to keep in touch.

➡ They write letters to businesses to compliment or complain about products or services or to request more information.

➡ Letters may be handwritten, typed and printed on the computer, mailed, or sent as e-mails to any place in the world.

➡ Autobiographical writing can include anecdotes, memorable events, life stories, and personal accounts of events.

➡ Blogs, social networking sites, and internet group forums can be a powerful form of personal writing that can be autobiographical, personal, or opinion-based in nature.

➡ Although texting uses its own set of abbreviations and phrases, it is still a way of expressing yourself through writing.

➡ Journaling allows writers to express personal thoughts and feelings privately. A journal can be a source for emotional release when feeling troubled, hurt, or lonely.

➡ Journal writing helps us to become more observant of ourselves and the world around us. Journaling allows us to exercise our imagination in words and pictures.

➡ Some types of personal writing, like letters, are meant to be shared with others. Journaling is often more private. What goes into your journal is up to you. It is also up to you whether or not you share your journal with others.

➡ Regular journal writing provides a written record you can use to go back and read again later. Writing in a journal while traveling helps remind you of what you saw and did. A journal is a place to store thoughts and ideas so they don't get lost.

   Some activities in this section involve writing journal entries. A journal can be any type of book with blank pages. It doesn't need to be fancy or expensive. You can write your journal in a spiral notebook, on theme paper in a three-ring binder, or even in a file on the computer.

1. Why do you think e-mail and texting have become so popular?

   _____

   _____

   _____

2. What types of things could you include in your journal?

   _____

   _____

   _____

Journaling

What should you write about in your journal? Anything you want. Stumped for writing ideas? Here's a few to get you started:

- The place I would most like to visit is ... because ...

- The person I most admire is ... because ...

- If I were an animal, I would be a ... because ...

- The most unique thing about me is ...

- To me, friendship means ...

- The thing that upsets me the most is ...

- The ten things I would most like to have are ...

- The most important lesson I ever learned was ...

- Last night, I dreamed that ...

- A skill I would really like to have is to be able to ...

- If I had $10,000, I would ...

- I feel afraid when ... because ...

- If I could invent something, it would be ...

- ◆ Besides writing in your journal, you could doodle or draw pictures.

- ◆ If you find a picture or cartoon in a magazine or on the Internet that you like, you could cut it out or print it and add it to your journal. It may become a writing idea.

- ◆ You could write the words to a song you like or a quotation by a famous person—or even one by someone who is not famous.

- ◆ When you think of good writing ideas, save them in your journal. Jot them down before they float off and dissolve like a wispy cloud on a windy day.

Write a journal entry using any of the ideas on this page. Also, save this page for another time when you need an idea.

Name: _____ Date: _____

Autobiography: All About You

An **autobiography** is a true account that a person writes about his or her life. It can include major events or focus on one specific event.

An autobiography can be about a person's whole life. It can be about one period in a person's life, such as childhood or a term as president. It can also be about one important day, or even about one important event, like meeting a celebrity, winning a contest, or witnessing an accident.

List ideas for each topic you could use for an autobiographical essay.

1. A special holiday: _____

    _____

2. An important day in your life: _____

    _____

3. A time you were proud of yourself: _____

    _____

4. Your bravest deed: _____

    _____

5. The ten best things about yourself: _____

    _____

6. An unusual day in your life: _____

    _____

7. The most valuable lesson you have learned in your life: _____

    _____

    _____

    _____

8. Use any of your ideas to write an autobiography on your own paper.

9. When you finish the rough draft, edit, revise, and proofread before writing the final version. If possible, add pictures or photographs.

Name: _____ Date: _____

Then and Now

How much have you changed in the past five years? What skills have you learned? What new experiences have you had? Have you moved to a new city or transferred to a new school? How have you changed physically?

You may also be the same in many ways as you were five years ago. Your favorite color or sport may be the same. You may live in the same house or have the same best friend.

1. Fill in the blanks with words and phrases to use for writing ideas. Continue on the next page.

Ways I've stayed the same	**Ways I've changed**
Physical:	
_____	_____
_____	_____
Where I live:	
_____	_____
_____	_____
What I enjoy doing in my spare time:	
_____	_____
_____	_____
My friends:	
_____	_____
_____	_____
My family:	
_____	_____
_____	_____
Where I go to school:	
_____	_____
_____	_____
Hobbies I enjoy:	
_____	_____
_____	_____

Name: _____   Date: _____

Then and Now (cont.)

	Ways I've stayed the same	**Ways I've changed**

Foods I like:

_____   _____

_____   _____

Books I like:

_____   _____

_____   _____

My personality:

_____   _____

_____   _____

Skills I have:

_____   _____

_____   _____

My most treasured possession:

_____   _____

_____   _____

How I interact with others:

_____   _____

_____   _____

Things that make me happy:

_____   _____

_____   _____

2. Use your ideas to compare and contrast yourself today to yourself five years ago, and write the comparison/contrast on your own paper. Include at least one paragraph about the ways in which you are the same as you were then and one paragraph about the ways in which you are different.

3. When you finish the first draft, proofread, edit, revise, and rewrite on your own paper. If possible, include a photograph of yourself, then and now.

Name: _____   Date: _____

An Unforgettable Meeting

Imagine having a once-in-a-lifetime chance to meet someone very special. If you could meet anyone who ever lived, past or present, any characters from any book or movie, or an alien from the other side of the galaxy, who would it be?

1. Who would you most like to meet? _____

2. Why? _____

   _____

3. If you could tell that person one thing about yourself, what would it be? _____

   _____

   _____

4. Describe how you would feel about meeting this person. _____

   _____

   _____

5. Write five questions you would most like to ask this person.

   a. _____

      _____

   b. _____

      _____

   c. _____

      _____

   d. _____

      _____

   e. _____

      _____

6. Write a newspaper headline in six words or less to describe your meeting.

   _____

   _____

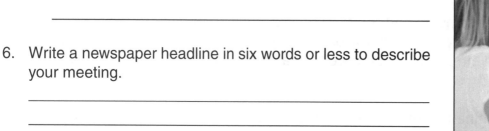

Blogs: Public Journals

Blogs, which is short for "web logs," are a new way for people to express their personal thoughts and opinions. For many **bloggers**, or people who blog, blogs are a kind of journal that is posted on the Internet for anyone to read. Blogs can be whatever you want them to be about. People write personal blogs about their everyday life, such as funny things that happen to them or what they cook for dinner. Other people write more professional blogs, such as blogs that review new cars or discuss new laws. Still other people write opinion blogs, where they post on topics they believe strongly in, such as saving the environment or spending money on education and after-school programs. No matter what kind of topic you are interested in, there is probably a blog about it.

Blogs can be a great way to express your feelings. Many blogs also allow for readers to post a comment, meaning you can have a conversation about your blog with your readers. There's no better way to get feedback on your writing than to have someone post a comment on it. Blogs are also permanent records of what you were feeling and thinking at any given time. You can go back and reread old blogs at any time.

When writing or reading a blog, it is important to remember that blogs are personal writing, first and foremost. It's your blog; you can write about whatever is important to you, just like in a journal.

The second most important thing to remember about blogs is that anyone can read it—your friends, family, teachers, even your parents' bosses could read it. Complete strangers can read your blog just as easily as your best friend can. There are some good guidelines to keep in mind as you write a blog:

✎ Decide how much you want to reveal. Do you want to use your real name? Maybe you or your parents would be more comfortable if you used a nickname, your initials, or a pen name.

✎ Post only appropriate material. A good rule of thumb is, if you don't want your mother to read it, don't post it.

✎ Be careful posting pictures of yourself. Do you or your parents really want complete strangers to know what you look like?

✎ Do not post photos you would not want your grandmother to see.

✎ Do not post photos or other information about your friends or family without their permission.

✎ Do not post certain information, such as your home or school address or phone number. Again, complete strangers can read your blog.

✎ Be polite. Because a blog is a public document, if you call someone an idiot, they will find out. If you wouldn't say it to their face, don't post it!

Letters: Keep in Touch

People write friendly letters to say thank you for a gift or favor, to invite a friend to an event, or to simply keep in touch. Many friendly letters are now sent by e-mail rather than regular mail (sometimes called snail mail).

When you write a friendly letter, imagine that you are talking to the person. Write your letter the way you would speak to the person if he or she were in the same room with you.

Whether you send them snail mail or e-mail, letters to friends and relatives should be fun and interesting for the reader.

1. Select one of the ideas below or one of your own. Write a letter on your own paper or use your computer to write an e-mail.

   ✎ Send a thank you for a gift or a special favor.

   ✎ Invite someone for a visit.

   ✎ Describe a trip you took.

   ✎ Describe a movie you saw or a book you read that you think the person might enjoy.

   ✎ Write about something that happened in school.

   ✎ Congratulate someone for something special they did recently.

   ✎ Describe your new home or school if you've recently moved.

   ✎ Write to your favorite author, musician, actor, or actress.

   ✎ Request an autograph from your favorite athlete. Include information about yourself and why you are interested in that sport.

   ✎ Write a thank-you letter to a parent for doing such a good job raising you.

   ✎ Describe an unusual weather event, like a blizzard, thunderstorm, or tornado, that you have experienced.

2. Take a few minutes to proofread your letter before you send it. Make sure you spelled words correctly, used proper grammar and punctuation, and wrote in complete sentences. Make corrections and rewrite if necessary.

Name: _____ Date: _____

Business Letters: Thank You for the Wonderful Service

People write business letters to request information, state opinions, express complaints, or send compliments. People are quick to complain, but they rarely remember to let others know when something is right.

1. Think about an item you recently received that works well or a place where you shopped, visited, or ate that offered friendly, helpful service.

   A. Describe the item or service that pleased you. _____

   _____

   B. Include details of the product, place, or service (who, what, when, and where).

   _____

   _____

   _____

   C. Give a specific example. _____

   _____

   _____

2. Use your ideas to write a complimentary letter to a company. You can find many addresses in the telephone book or on the Internet.
3. Address your letter to a specific person if possible (Ms. Goose, Dr. Bones, Professor Ivy). If not, use a job title, like Manager, Director, etc.
4. Type your letter using the format below for a business letter.

> Your name
> Your street address
> Your city, state, and zip code
> Today's date
>
> Name of person you are writing to, if known
> Company name
> Company street address
> Company city, state, and zip code
>
> Dear _____:
>
>   Body of letter
>
>   Yours truly,
>
>   Your name

Electronic Media

Today, more people than ever use the Internet to communicate. E-mail is short for electronic mail and is widely used. People also communicate through social networking sites such as Facebook or Myspace, text-messaging on their phones, and also Twitter, which allows people to post up to 140 characters about whatever they like. Electronic media users can write letters and even read books from their phones. New ways to communicate electronically are constantly being developed.

Whether you are sending an e-mail, updating your status, or reading a 'tweet,' you are communicating through writing. What separates these kinds of communications from business letters or persuasive reports? In many instances, people relax the grammar or spelling rules they use in e-mails. They may not capitalize proper nouns or check to make sure every word is spelled correctly. When people send text messages over their phones or post 'tweets,' they often use an understood set of abbreviations, such as "LOL" for "laughing out loud." The use of emoticons, or smiley faces, like :) for example, is also common.

There are several things to keep in mind when communicating with electronic media. The first is that not everyone will understand abbreviations, smiley faces, or other slang. If you are sending an e-mail to your grandmother, she may not understand that "BRB" means "be right back." So it is important to keep your reader in mind. You want to use words and phrases your reader will understand.

The second thing to keep in mind is that, even if your reader understands what "LOL" means, that does not make it appropriate in all settings. If you are sending an e-mail to the principal of your school, you should take a few extra minutes to make sure you are using proper grammar, capitalization and punctuation, and appropriate language. Read through your e-mail before you send it to make sure it is appropriate for the reader.

The third thing to remember is that once something is sent electronically, it never goes away. A permanent electronic record exists, and these records can be traced and searched. Text messages, e-mails, photographs taken with cell phones, and blog postings have all been used as evidence in court. So be selective in what you send electronically. A good rule of thumb is, if you wouldn't want your mother to see or read it, don't send it.

Mark "T" for True or "F" for false.

1. _____ Many people communicate using electronic media.

2. _____ Grammar and spelling do not matter in e-mail.

3. _____ Everyone understands what :) and :(mean.

4. _____ It is important to use words and phrases your reader will understand.

5. _____ 'Tweeting' is not a form of writing.

6. _____ You can write anything you want in a text message because no one will ever see it again.

7. _____ If you don't want your mother to read it, don't send it.

8. _____ Writers often relax grammar and spelling rules when using electronic media.

Name: _____   Date: _____

Time to Review: Personal Writing

Use the words in the box to help you identify the statements related to personal writing below. Write the correct term on the blank after each statement.

1. Things people want to accomplish

    _____

2. Short narrative about an interesting event

    _____

3. Feelings _____

4. A type of writing people use to compliment, complain, or request information

    _____

5. A way to privately express thoughts and feelings

    _____

6. Short for "web log" _____

7. A type of writing people use to invite, thank, or keep in touch with someone

    _____

8. Forms of communication including blogs, e-mails, social networking sites, and tweets

    _____

9. Letters written on a computer and sent over the Internet

    _____

10. Rhyming phrase to describe regular mail _____

11. An account a person writes about his or her life _____

12. People who write blogs _____

| emotions |
| snail mail |
| electronic media |
| business letter |
| goals |
| e-mail |
| bloggers |
| journaling |
| autobiography |
| anecdote |
| blog |
| friendly letter |

Descriptive Writing

Descriptive writing provides vivid details. The key to a good description is to be as specific as possible.

The main purpose of a description is to enable the reader to picture what you're describing. These tips will help you to write better descriptions.

Decide on a topic: Before you begin writing, decide on a topic. If your topic is too broad, you may not be able to cover it completely. If your topic is too narrow, you may not have enough to write about.

Gather ideas: This can include jotting down ideas, checking reference sources, doing surveys, gathering data, etc.

Organize your material: Describing events in order works best for many topics. It provides a time sense of what happened first, next, and last. You can also outline your topic and organize the main ideas in order of importance, with examples or explanations for each main point.

Add details, descriptions, and examples: Details related to the main topic provide the reader with a clear image.

Edit and revise: When you finish your first draft, ask yourself:

- Is my writing clear and concise?
- Is any important information missing?
- Is there too much or too little detail?
- Did I use complete sentences?
- Did I stick to my topic?
- Did I include an interesting topic sentence and conclusion?

Proofread: Correct errors in grammar, punctuation, and spelling.

Double-check: Go back and read through your final copy one more time.

Name: _____   Date: _____

Topic Sentences: A Delicious Paragraph

A **paragraph** is a group of sentences about a specific topic. An interesting paragraph is like a tasty sandwich.

When you bite into a sandwich, the top piece of bread is the first thing you taste. The **topic sentence** of a paragraph is like the top piece of bread. It introduces the main idea of a paragraph. If the topic sentence is not fresh and interesting, the reader won't want to bite any further.

Interesting topic sentences encourage readers to bite further into the paragraph.

Write two different topic sentences for each subject.

1. a trip in a canoe _____
   _____
   _____
   _____
   _____

2. being lost in a forest _____
   _____
   _____
   _____
   _____

3. taking care of a pet _____
   _____
   _____
   _____
   _____

4. a person you admire _____
   _____
   _____
   _____
   _____

5. Save this page to use with the next activity.

Name: _____ Date: _____

Supporting Sentences: The Tasty Filling

A great slice of bread alone does not make a memorable sandwich. The middle of the sandwich needs to include interesting and tasty ingredients.

Topic sentences are followed by **supporting sentences** that provide interesting information, give examples, or provide additional details and descriptions.

1. Write two sentences that could follow each topic sentence.

    As soon as I woke up, I knew it was going to be one of those days when nothing goes right.

    _____

    _____

    _____

    _____

    _____

    As darkness crept toward us, we huddled closer to the fire, listening to the sounds of the waking forest.

    _____

    _____

    _____

    _____

    _____

2. Rewrite your best topic sentence from the last activity. Add supporting sentences.

    _____

    _____

    _____

    _____

    _____

    _____

    _____

    _____

3. Save this page to use with the next activity.

Name: _____ Date: _____

Concluding Sentences: Good to the Last Bite

The bottom piece of bread in a sandwich is like the **conclusion sentence** in a paragraph. Without the second piece of bread, the sandwich would fall apart. The conclusion sentence restates the main idea or sums up the main points in a paragraph.

1. Write a conclusion sentence for one of the three topics on the last page.

   _____

   _____

   _____

2. Cut out a picture from an old magazine that shows any type of scenery, preferably one without people. The scene could be of a city, mountain, rain forest, or even under the ocean. Imagine visiting this place.

3. Write a topic sentence you could use to begin a paragraph describing your visit to the place shown in the picture.

   _____

   _____

4. List details you might see, hear, feel, taste, and touch if you were there in person.

   _____

   _____

   _____

5. Write a conclusion sentence to sum up a paragraph about your visit to this place.

   _____

   _____

   _____

6. On your own paper, write a descriptive paragraph about any person, place, thing, or event. You can use any of the topics or sentences you wrote about in the last two activities.

7. Reread what you wrote. Keep these questions in mind as you revise your descriptive paragraph.

   • Can you make the topic sentence more interesting?
   • Did you include descriptions, details, and/or examples in the middle of the paragraph?
   • Did your conclusion sum up the main idea of the paragraph?

Name: _____　Date: _____

Be Wise, Capitalize

Part of good writing is checking for words that should (and should not) be capitalized. Proper capitalization makes it easier for the reader to understand your point.

Fill in the blanks with more examples. Always capitalize:

- The first word of every sentence

- The word *I*, as in "I am home."

- Titles of people: Mr.; Dr.; President

  _____

- Names of specific people: George Washington; Anne Frank

  _____

- Names of specific places: Lincoln Tunnel; Kennedy Expressway

  _____

- Names of specific buildings: Eiffel Tower; Empire State Building

  _____

- Names of special documents: Declaration of Independence

  _____

- Important words in titles of books, movies, newspapers, and magazines: *Gone With the Wind; Harry Potter and the Sorcerer's Stone*

  _____

- Cities, counties, states, and countries: Paris; Ohio; Japan

  _____

- Names of lakes, rivers, mountains, and oceans: Lake Winnebago; Pacific Ocean

  _____

- Historical events: Boxer Rebellion; Civil War

  _____

- Names of clubs and organizations: Girl Scouts; Salvation Army

  _____

- Brand names: Lego™; Kleenex™

  _____

- Proper adjectives: Mexican; Greek; Hawaiian

  _____

Name: _____ Date: _____

To Capitalize or Not to Capitalize? ... That Is the Question

1. Cross out the words in the list that should not be capitalized.

2. Look up, down, backward, forward, and diagonally to find and circle in the puzzle only the words that should be capitalized. (*Hint:* 30 words can be found in the puzzle.)

apple
avenue
bible
canada
capital
china
constitution
dad
donna
dr. jones
grade
greece
harry
high school
japan
july
king lear
lassie
leon
lindsey
man
mexico
miguel
mother
mouse
museum
ohio
paris

T	P	N	W	L	U	A	P	S	A	L	T	L	A	K	E	J	B	T	M
N	V	K	Y	M	N	T	K	L	L	C	H	I	N	A	N	J	L	E	K
O	C	Q	F	K	J	S	I	W	R	E	J	C	S	M	A	P	V	X	G
I	R	R	Y	P	T	N	P	L	V	W	U	L	Q	P	P	W	N	A	K
H	T	M	L	L	D	G	H	I	W	T	F	G	K	R	A	P	M	S	P
O	E	M	C	S	A	R	K	L	D	W	C	T	I	Z	J	I	T	R	D
N	L	G	E	O	X	S	E	C	E	E	R	G	A	M	R	Q	N	R	D
Z	B	Y	N	Y	N	F	S	Y	L	V	R	D	W	J	V	G	.	T	N
B	I	L	L	I	Z	S	A	I	P	V	A	M	W	H	K	J	X	E	D
G	B	U	F	T	V	D	T	R	E	N	W	H	A	M	O	W	F	K	O
H	J	Q	M	X	S	I	T	I	A	Q	I	B	M	N	R	A	M	A	N
L	F	R	L	E	H	C	G	C	T	T	H	Y	E	N	L	L	R	L	N
F	M	H	U	N	G	K	M	S	E	U	Y	S	R	G	M	L	N	N	A
A	L	T	L	N	T	X	L	H	K	L	T	R	V	M	N	S	H	U	C
E	L	T	L	L	R	C	O	N	R	N	V	I	R	D	R	T	M	S	W
S	E	Y	T	S	F	U	X	Z	K	W	A	Q	O	A	B	R	G	Q	L
D	O	F	I	H	S	K	W	L	P	M	V	H	R	N	H	E	M	H	Y
E	N	R	T	E	O	C	I	X	E	M	R	M	T	H	Z	E	X	P	L
R	A	N	R	P	F	K	R	Z	Z	Z	T	S	E	A	T	T	L	E	K
P	V	L	T	X	K	I	N	G	L	E	A	R	R	P	R	W	L	V	L

park   paul   queen   red sea   salt lake
seattle   seven   sister   son   spain
spiderman   street   summer   sun lake   teacher
texas   thanksgiving three   tuesday   wall street
white house   winter   woman

Name: _____ Date: _____

See It!

When you write, you become the eyes of the reader. Descriptive writing uses adjectives to provide the reader with a clear picture of people, places, things, and ideas. Sight words include descriptions of color, shape, size, and texture.

Each of these phrases describes a type of container. Read the description, then draw the container. Use colored pencils or pens.

1. a rotten, wooden chest with rusted hinges

2. a green and red plastic toy box

3. a large, shiny, metal safe

4. a square, battered cardboard box

5. an empty, rectangular glass aquarium

6. a triangular stone pyramid

7. Decide on an object to describe. On your own paper, write a paragraph describing that object in detail, but do not name the object. Call it "Object X" if you need to use a word. Describe the size, shape, color, texture, and other features of the object.

8. When you finish your paragraph, trade papers with a partner. Read each other's descriptions. See if you can guess the object being described.

Name: _____ Date: _____

Hear It!

Sounds are everywhere. What do you hear when you close your eyes and listen? Can you hear the motor on your refrigerator? The hum of your computer? Traffic noises? Children playing? Birds singing?

Buzz, creak, howl, roar, cheer, rumble, crash, and *squeak* describe sounds. **Onomatopoeia** uses words that imitate a sound. The words can be real, like *crunch*, or made-up, like *ka-pow* and *ka-boom*.

Write words to describe these sounds. You can use real words or make up your own.

1. Walking barefoot through squishy mud _____

_____

_____

2. A rocky shore with huge waves crashing _____

_____

_____

3. Going down a huge waterslide _____

_____

_____

4. What you hear right now if you close your eyes and listen _____

_____

_____

5. On your own paper, describe an experience so that the reader can hear the sounds of the event. (Experiences could be attending the circus, playing football, watching a parade, walking down a busy city street, or sitting at an airport.)

6. When you finish, proofread, edit, revise, and rewrite your description.

Name: _____   Date: _____

Smell It!

Imagine watching a movie that provided not only sound and pictures, but also smells! Describing smells in writing adds to the reader's sense of being part of the scene.

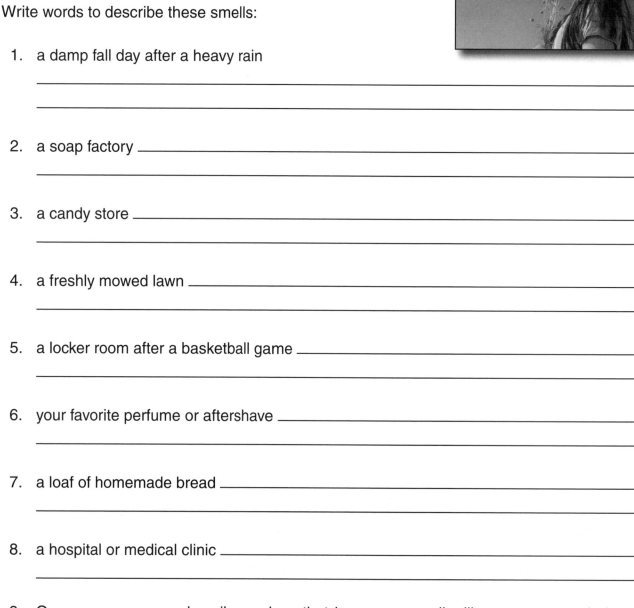

Write words to describe these smells:

1. a damp fall day after a heavy rain

   _____

   _____

2. a soap factory _____

   _____

3. a candy store _____

   _____

4. a freshly mowed lawn _____

   _____

5. a locker room after a basketball game _____

   _____

6. your favorite perfume or aftershave _____

   _____

7. a loaf of homemade bread _____

   _____

8. a hospital or medical clinic _____

   _____

9. On your own paper, describe a place that has many smells, like a restaurant, bakery, kitchen, or garden. Use sensory words that describe the various aromas.

10. When you finish, proofread, edit, revise, and rewrite your description.

Did You Know? Movies with "Smell-O-Vision" were first introduced in 1960, but they never became popular.

Name: _____ Date: _____

Taste It!

Imagine eating a bowl of cold, creamy, mint chocolate ice cream on a hot summer day. *Cold, creamy, mint,* and *chocolate* describe the taste, temperature, and texture of the ice cream. *Sweet, hot, sour, crunchy, tangy, salty,* and *bitter* are other adjectives that describe taste and texture.

1. Write taste, temperature, and texture words to describe each item.

    A. stale bread _____

    _____

    B. a cup of hot cocoa with marshmallows _____

    _____

    C. a steaming bowl of spicy chili _____

    _____

    D. a two-day-old deluxe pizza with 10 toppings _____

    _____

    E. mashed potatoes and gravy _____

    _____

2. List six fruit flavors. _____

    _____

3. List six vegetable flavors. _____

    _____

4. List six words that describe the texture of food.

    _____

    _____

5. On your own paper, describe your favorite meal so that the reader will be able to "taste" all the goodies.

6. When you finish, proofread, edit, revise, and rewrite your description.

Name: _____ Date: _____

Touch It!

We use our hands to feel the texture of objects. Sandpaper feels rough and gritty. *Bumpy, smooth, wet, warm,* and *soft* are other words that describe how something feels.

Your sense of touch is not limited to your hands. Cold rain on your face, the wind blowing through your hair, the hot sun beating on your skin, and walking barefoot through thick, cool, squishy mud are also sensory experiences.

List words to describe these experiences.

1. cuddling with a fuzzy blanket _____

   _____

2. walking on a cold, windy, rainy day_____

   _____

3. lifting a heavy wooden box _____

   _____

4. running a long race _____

   _____

5. jumping into cold water _____

   _____

Most experiences involve using several senses at the same time.

6. Which senses would you use if you were a drummer in a marching band?

   _____

   _____

7. Which senses would you use if you were chopping onions?

   _____

   _____

8. On your own paper, describe a personal experience so the reader can share the feel and texture of the event. (Experiences could be falling asleep in a hammock, wading in a creek, or standing on a hill on a windy day.)

9. When you finish, proofread, edit, revise, and rewrite your description.

Show Me in Words

1. On your own paper, write a paragraph to describe one of these scenes. Use sensory words to paint a picture of the sights, sounds, smells, tastes, and feel of the scene.

    At the circus: A visit to a circus involves the use of all of your senses as you watch the clowns, hear the elephants, smell the popcorn, taste the cotton candy, and feel its stickiness on your face.

    Visit a deli: Describe a visit to a busy neighborhood deli around noon when people are ordering lunch and drinks. What do you see, hear, smell, taste, and touch?

    At the beach: Describe the sights, sounds, smells, tastes, and feel of a trip to a crowded beach on a day when the temperature is close to 100 degrees Fahrenheit.

    In your neighborhood: Imagine taking your orange juice and toast outside early in the morning after a rainy night. Use sensory words to describe what you see, hear, taste, smell, and feel as you sit on the front steps.

    Brrr!: Although the sun is shining, the temperature is only around 20 degrees Fahrenheit. Describe what it would be like to build a snowman or go sledding, skating, or skiing on a bright winter day.

    Clues to the Chocolate Chip Cookie Caper: Imagine being the first police officer at the scene of a robbery in a bakery. Someone stole all of the chocolate chip cookies! Use sensory words to describe what you see, hear, taste, smell, and feel as you investigate the crime and look for clues.

2. When you finish your first draft, edit, revise, and proofread your paragraph. Draw a picture to go with your paragraph, or use computer clip art to create a scene.

Name: _____ Date: _____

Happy, Sad, Proud, Rejected

Everyone has emotions. **Emotions** are all the different feelings we experience. Emotions can be happy and pleasant; emotions can also be sad or scary.

Define each emotion by giving an example below. The first one has been done for you.

1. I feel **angry** when someone yells at me for no reason.

2. I feel **happy** when _____
   _____

3. I feel **sad** when _____
   _____

4. I feel **proud** when _____
   _____

5. I feel **rejected** when _____
   _____

6. I feel **afraid** when _____
   _____

7. I feel **confident** when _____
   _____

8. I feel **lonely** when _____
   _____

9. I feel **jealous** when _____
   _____
   _____

10. Think about a time when you had strong feelings
    about something. It could be a time when you were
    feeling very good or very bad. Write in your journal
    about what happened to make you feel that way.

Name: _____ Date: _____

A Perfect Day

Imagine planning a perfect day: one that involved doing whatever you wanted with your favorite people, going anyplace you wanted, and eating your favorite foods.

Write a plan for your perfect day.

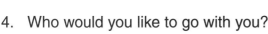

1. What would the weather be like?

_____

_____

_____

2. Where would you spend the day?

_____

_____

_____

3. What would you do there? _____

_____

_____

_____

_____

_____

_____

4. Who would you like to go with you? _____

_____

5. What would you eat? _____

_____

_____

6. What else would make this day perfect? _____

_____

_____

_____

_____

_____

Name: _____ Date: _____

Relationships

Every day, we interact with family members, friends, classmates, and other people. Some relationships may be smooth and enjoyable. Other relationships may be stormy. Writing about relationships with other people can provide many journaling opportunities.

Think of someone you get along with very well. Do you have a lot in common with that person? Are you a lot alike? Do you enjoy doing the same things?

1. Write why you think you get along well with this person. _____
    _____
    _____
    _____

2. List three adjectives that describe your personality. _____
    _____

3. List three adjectives that describe the personality of people you like. _____
    _____

4. List three adjectives that describe personality traits of people you don't get along with.
    _____
    _____

Is there a member of your family or class that you have not been able to get along with very well?

5. In your journal, write about someone you don't get along with very well, and why you think there is a problem. List three things you could try doing to get along better with this person.

6. Try at least one of your ideas. If that doesn't work, try the others. Really try. In your journal, write about how well your ideas worked.

Name: _____ Date: _____

Synonyms: Pretty Flowers + Pretty Garden = Pretty Dull

Most people wouldn't want to eat the same foods at every meal. That would be very dull! They wouldn't want to watch the same movie or read the same book over and over, either. People enjoy variety.

Variety makes your writing more interesting. **Synonyms** are words that mean the same, or nearly the same, thing. You can find synonyms for many words in a **thesaurus**.

Write two or more synonyms for each word. Use a thesaurus if you need ideas.

1. run _____

2. saw _____

3. heard _____

4. funny _____

5. strange _____

6. nice _____

7. tame _____

8. loud _____

9. exciting _____

In the following paragraph, the word *pretty* is used five times. Dull and boring! Rewrite the paragraph, and replace the word *pretty* with five different words. Change any other words that you think are dull.

10. Rachel wandered happily through the pretty garden. She had never seen so many pretty flowers in her life. Some were so pretty that they looked like rainbows. The pretty flowers in the pretty garden had as many colors as a box of 64 crayons.

_____

_____

_____

_____

_____

_____

_____

Name: _____   Date: _____

Finish the Pictures

"His eyes—how they twinkled! His dimples how merry!
His cheeks were like roses, his nose like a cherry!
His droll little mouth was drawn up like a bow,
And the beard on his chin was as white as the snow."

"He had a broad face and a little round belly,
That shook when he laughed like a bowlful of jelly.
He was chubby and plump …"

Even if you had never seen a picture of him, this description from the poem "A Visit from St. Nicholas" would enable most people to visualize St. Nicholas (Santa Claus).

Finish each drawing using the description provided.

1. Her hair looked like a frizzy dandelion gone to seed.

2. His eyes were set close together, giving him a sinister look.

3. As soon as I saw his huge grin and the laugh lines around his eyes, I knew I'd like James.

4. The manticore was a Greek mythological beast with a human face and ears, blue eyes, and three rows of sharp teeth in each jaw. It had the body and tail of a lion with a ball of poisoned spines on the end.

Name: _____　Date: _____

Paint a Word Picture

　　　Would you be able to describe someone well enough for an artist to draw a picture of that person?

Use words and phrases to describe the features and physical characteristics of someone you know well, like a parent, friend, brother, sister, or other relative.

Male or female? _____

Age: _____　　Height: _____

Weight: _____　　Skin color: _____　　Eye color: _____

Describe hair color and style: _____

_____

Describe the eyebrows: _____

Describe the nose: _____

Describe the mouth: _____

Describe the ears: _____

Does this person have pierced ears? One, or both? _____

Does he or she wear glasses? If so, describe them. _____

_____

What else is unique about the person's face? _____

_____

What type of clothing does this person usually wear? _____

_____

Describe any type of jewelry (rings, watch, necklace, earrings, etc.) this person usually wears.

_____

What would most people notice about this person if he or she were in a group of people about

the same age? _____

_____

Describe the way this person walks. _____

Describe this person's voice. _____

Save this page to use with the next activity.

Name: _____ Date: _____

Options Available

A picture of a person could be a realistic photograph, a cartoon drawing, or an abstract painting. It could also be an action shot or a portrait. The picture could be done in pencil, charcoal, paint, or crayon.

Writing about a person can also be done in many different ways.

➡ You could write a physical description of someone.

➡ You could describe that person's character traits or focus on one particular trait, such as generosity or bravery.

➡ You could write about a particular memory you have of that person.

➡ You could write a humorous anecdote about someone.

➡ You could write a poem about him or her.

➡ You could make that person the main character in a play or short story.

➡ You could write a dialogue between yourself and that person.

➡ You could write him or her a letter.

➡ You could write a news article about something that person did.

1. Who will you write about? _____

2. Narrow your focus. What will be the main idea of your paragraph?

   _____

   _____

   _____

   _____

3. Write about that person on your own paper. Use any style of writing (essay, poetry, short story, etc.).

4. When you finish, edit, revise, and proofread your work. If possible, draw a picture or add a photograph of that person.

5. The person you wrote about would probably enjoy reading what you wrote. If you'd like, share your writing with him or her.

Name: _____   Date: _____

From Dull to Lively

Verbs are words that show action or being. Lively verbs like *trembled, whirled, shivered, frolicked*, and *screamed* make writing more interesting.

Use **lively verbs** to change dull sentences to interesting ones.

Dull: The dog was happy.
Interesting: The dog quivered with excitement.

Rewrite the sentences to make them more interesting by using action verbs.

1. He was sad. _____
    _____

2. The girl was scared. _____
    _____

3. Jason was hungry. _____
    _____

4. They were lonely. _____
    _____

5. They were jogging in the park. _____
    _____

6. "I am fine," Gavin said. _____
    _____

7. The child left the cold water. _____
    _____

8. The grass was green. _____
    _____

9. The sky was cloudy. _____
    _____

10. Yesterday was a nice day. _____
    _____

Name: _____ Date: _____

Marcus Roared With Laughter

Lively verbs like *dashed, squealed, quaked,* and *bubbled* create more interesting and more precise details for the reader. Lively verbs change dull sentences to interesting ones, and they provide a clearer picture of the action.

Dull: The child was afraid.   **More interesting:** The lost toddler shivered with fear.

Rewrite the sentences to make them more interesting by using action verbs and descriptive adjectives.

1. Tina was sad. _____
   _____

2. Tim was happy. _____
   _____

3. The snake made a noise. _____
   _____

4. They were hungry. _____
   _____

5. The cat and dog looked at each other. _____
   _____

6. "I am leaving," he said. _____
   _____

7. The thunder was loud. _____
   _____

8. The flowers had a nice smell. _____
   _____

9. The crowd was excited. _____
   _____

10. He ate his spinach. _____
    _____

Name: _____ Date: _____

Active Voice, Active Writing

Using the active voice in your writing helps the reader understand your point. **Active voice** is where the subject of your sentence is doing the action. Using active voice makes your writing easy to understand by clearly identifying the subject, verb, and object.

- Bob walked the dog. (*Bob* is the subject, *walked* is the active verb, and *the dog* is the object)

Passive voice is where the subject of your sentence has an action done to him. The subject is usually identified in a *by* phrase, which comes after the verb. The verb is usually the past participle form of *to be* plus the action verb.

- The dog was walked by Bob. (*the dog* is the object, *was walked* is the passive verb, and *by Bob* is the subject)

Passive voice is useful in several situations.

- Use passive voice when you do not know who the subject is.
  - The bike was stolen on Thursday. (*by someone* is understood)
- Use the passive voice when everyone understands who the subject is.
  - The thief was arrested on Friday. (*by the police* is understood, because the police are the only people who arrest thieves)
- Use the passive voice when you do not want to emphasize the subject in the sentence.
  - The thief was convicted by a jury of his peers. (This sentence could read *A jury of his peers convicted the thief*, but the writer wants to emphasize *the thief*, not *the jury*.)

In all other cases, using the active voice makes your writing stronger and easier to read.

Read the following sentences and mark "A" if they are active or "P" if they are passive.

1. _____ Larry mowed the lawn and raked the leaves.
2. _____ The trash was picked up on Tuesday.
3. _____ Milly was shocked by the news that she'd won the poetry contest.
4. _____ Janice wrote a thank you card to her grandmother.
5. _____ North America was discovered in 1492 by Christopher Columbus.
6. _____ Jorge was late to class because his lock was jammed.
7. _____ Susie will love the present I got for her.
8. _____ The dog left a trail of muddy paw prints throughout the house.
9. Choose one of the passive sentences above and rewrite it as an active sentence.

_____

_____

Ready, Set, Action!

By using **action verbs** and **descriptive adjectives** in your writing, your readers will understand events clearly and feel like they are part of the scene.

1. On your own paper, write a paragraph to describe one of the scenes below. Use sensory words, action verbs, active voice, sentence variety, and descriptive adjectives.

    A sporting event: Describe a sporting event like a track meet, football game, stock-car race, or volleyball tournament. Write about the experience from the point of view of either a participant or a fan.

    Loop-de-loop: Describe a wild ride on a huge roller coaster from the point of view of someone on the ride.

    At the Olympics: Imagine being at the Olympics. Write about the experience from the point of view of either a participant or a spectator.

    Family get-together: Describe the people and events at a large family holiday get-together.

    A day at the zoo or circus: A zoo is filled with many sights, sounds, and smells. Describe a visit to a zoo or circus.

    The first day of school: The first day of class can be exciting and confusing, especially if you are attending a new school. Describe your first day at school this year.

    Moving time: Packing, moving, unpacking, and getting organized can be a lot of hard work. Describe a move you've made to a different house.

2. When you finish your first draft, edit, revise, and proofread your paragraph.

Name: _____ Date: _____

As Stubborn as a Mule

Similes are figures of speech that compare two unlike objects using the words *like* or *as*. Similes provide descriptive pictures of people, places, and things.

Examples: Her smile was **like** sunshine on a cloudy day.
The old prospector's skin was **as** brown and wrinkled **as** a baked potato.

Finish the similes.

1.   The moon shone as brightly as _____.

2.   The fog enclosed us like _____.

3.   Her hair looked like _____.

4.   The cloud looked as fluffy as _____.

5.   They were as _____ as _____.

6.   She danced like a _____.

7.   Her smile was as welcome as _____.

8.   Grandpa's words made the boy feel as _____ as a

_____.

9.   _____ was like a winter blizzard.

10. _____ was as _____ as a nest of hornets.

Write three similes of your own.

11. _____

_____

12. _____

_____

13. _____

_____

Name: _____ Date: _____

A Streak of Lightning

Metaphors are figures of speech that compare two unlike objects without using the words *like* or *as*.

1. Circle the two objects being compared in each sentence.

   A. The coach's mood was a thunderstorm after the game.

   B. The trip across the desert was a nightmare of light and heat.

   C. The mall was a zoo on Saturdays.

   D. The fog was a cat creeping silently through the night.

   E. The eagle was a streak of lightning across the sky.

Both items in a metaphor must be **nouns**. "Josh is sad" is not a metaphor because *sad* is an adjective, not a noun.

2. Complete the metaphors.

   A. The heat was _____
                                    (noun)

   B. The north wind is _____
                                    (noun)

   C. Her loneliness was _____
                                    (noun)

   D. The ferocious storm was _____
                                    (noun)

   E. The restless children were _____
                                    (noun)

   F. The creaking door was _____
                                    (noun)

   G. The mall was _____ at midnight.
                          (noun)

3. Write a metaphor about a person. Circle both nouns.

   _____

   _____

4. Write a metaphor about an animal. Circle both nouns.

   _____

   _____

5. Write a metaphor about a weather-related event. Circle both nouns.

   _____

   _____

Name: _____ Date: _____

Opposites Attract

When writing comparison/contrast descriptions, you'll probably use many **antonyms**, which are words that have opposite meanings.

1. Write an antonym for each word. Use a dictionary or thesaurus if you need help.

angry _____	adult _____
bad _____	big _____
cold _____	catch _____
down _____	dull _____
end _____	exit _____
foolish _____	friendly _____
good _____	high _____
in _____	just _____
kind _____	laugh _____
love _____	major _____
me _____	noon _____
open _____	parent _____
please _____	put _____
quiet _____	sooner _____
sunny _____	true _____
ugly _____	up _____
windy _____	winner _____

2. Write 10 words to describe an elephant.

   _____

   _____

   _____

3. Write 10 words to describe a mouse.

   _____

   _____

   _____

Name: _____ Date: _____

Like Walking on Eggs

Idioms are phrases that say one thing but actually mean something else. Idioms should be used sparingly when writing.

Circle the idiom in each sentence, and then write a brief explanation of what is actually meant.

1. When the Johnsons adopted their baby, the process involved a lot of red tape.

    _____

    _____

2. Last Saturday, it rained cats and dogs.

    _____

    _____

3. Our cousins in Ireland rolled out the red carpet when we went for a visit.

    _____

    _____

4. Cassie was a bundle of nerves on the first day at her new school.

    _____

    _____

5. Jay had butterflies in his stomach when he gave his speech.

    _____

    _____

6. Maria felt down in the dumps when her turtle ran away.

    _____

    _____

7. "It's a secret," whispered Todd, "so button your lip."

    _____

    _____

8. Mom blew her stack when she saw the mess in the kitchen.

    _____

    _____

Name: _____   Date: _____

Words of Wisdom

Proverbs are short sayings that many people accept as true.

Where there's a will, there's a way.

Good things come to those who wait.

Actions speak louder than words.

Every cloud has a silver lining.

Look before you leap.

Treat others as you would like to be treated.

It's better to give than to receive.

Never judge a book by its cover.

Haste makes waste.

1.   Select one of the proverbs. Explain what it means to you. Write about something that happened to you that would be an example of that saying.

A stitch in time saves nine.

_____

_____

_____

_____

_____

_____

Half a loaf is better than none.

_____

Continue writing on your own paper if you need more room.

Name: _____ Date: _____

Time To Review: Descriptive Writing

Use the words in the box to complete the activity. Write the correct term on the line after each statement.

1. Figures of speech that compare two unlike objects using the

   words *like* or *as* _____

2. Phrases that say one thing, but actually mean something

   else _____

3. Words that describe nouns

   _____

4. Figures of speech that compare two unlike objects without

   using the words *like* or *as*

   _____

autobiography
proverb
topic sentence
similes
thesaurus
synonyms
metaphors
sensory words
idioms
paragraph
adjectives
conclusion
supporting sentences
antonyms

5. Words that mean the same, or nearly the same, thing _____

6. A sentence that sums up or restates the main idea of a paragraph

   _____

7. Words that describe senses _____

8. A book that lists synonyms _____

9. A group of sentences about a topic with a beginning, a middle, and a conclusion

   _____

10. Words that have opposite meanings _____

11. Sentences that provide descriptions, details, and examples

    _____

12. The first sentence of a paragraph _____

Name: _____ Date: _____

Many Types of Fiction

There are many types of **fictional stories** and many ways to write them. Authors usually write fiction to entertain or to teach lessons.

➡ Most young children enjoy **fairy tales** like "Cinderella" and "The Three Little Pigs."

➡ Stories of **fantasy** like the *Harry Potter* books often take place in magical places. Characters in fantasies can include elves, giants, trolls, wizards, animals, or magical objects.

➡ The best-known **fables** (stories that teach lessons) were written by Aesop. Animals or objects that act like people are usually the main characters.

➡ **Tall Tales** are humorous adventure stories featuring super characters like Paul Bunyan, John Henry, and Pecos Bill.

➡ Many readers enjoy **detective stories and mysteries**. The plots involve crimes or other puzzling events. Readers like to try to figure out "whodunit" before the author reveals the answer at the end of the story.

➡ **Science fiction** stories use scientific knowledge and specula-tion as a major part of the plot, setting, or theme. They may include inventions that are within the realm of future possibility but not yet available.

➡ **Historical stories** can be about real people or events that have occurred, but they may also include fictional characters, dialogue, and events.

➡ **Myths** are stories about gods, heroes, animals, or events. Often, they explain a natural event, like why we have winter. Myths also instruct and entertain.

1. What was your favorite fairy tale? _____

2. Who is your favorite tall-tale character? _____

3. What type of stories do you like best? _____

   Why? _____

   _____

   _____

   _____

Name: _____ Date: _____

Writing Beginnings: Once Upon a Time

A story with a **good beginning** grabs the attention of readers so they want to continue reading. Avoid weak or dull sentences when you write.

Directions: Give a reason why you think each sentence would or would not be a good beginning for a story.

1. Until today, no one except me has known the truth of what really happened that night twenty years ago when Riverside Mansion went up in flames.

   _____

   _____

2. "You found a *what*?" screamed Jake. "Where did you find it?"

   _____

3. Lisa got up in the morning and looked out the window, and she was happy because it wasn't raining.

   _____

4. "Follow me," Rachel whispered. She turned to look at her friends. "If we get caught ..." she began and stopped suddenly. She was now alone in the cave, except that she could hear the sound of the stranger's footsteps growing louder.

   _____

5. I want to tell you a story about my Uncle Will and his pets. _____

   _____

6. He had two dogs, a cat, three hamsters, a parrot, and a snake. _____

   _____

Directions: Rewrite these weak sentences to make them more interesting.

7. Yesterday, I walked home from school. _____

   _____

8. Jason met a dragon on his way to the library. _____

   _____

9. Cinderella had a mean stepmother and two stepsisters who did not treat her very well.

   _____

   _____

   _____

Name: _____   Date: _____

Describing Characters: Curly Hair and Laughing Eyes

All short stories include a **main character**. The main character could be a person, animal, or object. Characters can be realistic or completely imaginary.

Physical characteristics describe how a person looks. Even if you aren't planning to use all of the information in a story, it helps to paint a complete picture of the character clearly in your mind.

Does your character have tight dark curls or hair that looks like it's been struck by lightning? Does your character have a bump on his nose, or scabs on her knees? Does she have beautiful brown eyes?

Describe two people you might use as characters in a story.

	Male character	**Female character**
Age:	_____	_____
Height:	_____	_____
Weight:	_____	_____
Eyes:	_____	_____
Nose:	_____	_____
Mouth:	_____	_____
Hairstyle/color:	_____	_____
Complexion:	_____	_____
Voice:	_____	_____
Manner of speaking:	_____	_____
Type of laugh:	_____	_____
Manner of walking:	_____	_____
More details:	_____	_____
	_____	_____
	_____	_____
	_____	_____

Save your ideas to use in a future story.

Name: _____ Date: _____

Guess Who?: Describing Characters

Select the picture of a person you might use as a character in a story. Fill in the blanks about that character on the next page.

A.

B.

C.

D.

E.

F.

G.

H.

I.

J.

K.

L.

Name: _____ Date: _____

Guess Who?: Describing Characters (cont.)

1. What is the character's name? _____

2. What is this person's favorite hobby? _____

3. What is this person's occupation? If the character is a child, what occupation would he/ she like to have someday?

    _____

4. What is this person's favorite food? _____

5. What is this person's favorite beverage?_____

6. What type of pet does this person have, and what is the pet's name? _____

    _____

7. What is this person's best quality? _____

8. What is this person's favorite sport? _____

9. What is this person's worst bad habit? _____

10. What does this person dislike most? _____

    _____

11. What time of day does this person like best? _____

12. What does this person like to do most on a Sunday morning? _____

    _____

13. Where does this person live? Describe it. _____

    _____

14. Where does this person like to go on vacation? _____

    _____

15. What does this person like to do to relax? _____

    _____

16. Why would you like to have this person as a friend? _____

    _____

Get together with a small group. Read your answers. Let other members of the group try to guess which character you selected. Save your character ideas for use in a future story.

Name: _____ Date: _____

Creating People Characters: A Laugh Like a Hyena

Do you know anyone with an unusual talent, a peculiar laugh, or a funny way of dancing? How about friends or family members with unique hobbies or pets? Even the clearest photograph won't reveal information like honesty, bravery, generosity, or fear of snakes.

You can combine bits and pieces of people you know, characters you've read about, or ones you've seen in movies to **create completely new characters**.

1. Write words and phrases to describe one of the main characters from *The Wizard of Oz*—Dorothy, the Tin Man, the Scarecrow, or the Cowardly Lion. _____
   _____
   _____

2. Write words and phrases to describe a favorite relative. _____
   _____
   _____

3. Write words and phrases to describe yourself. _____
   _____
   _____

4. Write words and phrases to describe your favorite fictional character. _____
   _____
   _____

Combine your ideas to create a new character: a twelve-year-old boy or girl who wakes up in the morning on a different planet.

5. What is the first thing your character would say? _____
   _____
   _____

6. What is the first thing your character would do? _____
   _____
   _____

7. How does your character react when he or she hears a knock at the door?
   _____
   _____
   _____

8. What does your character want to do next? _____
   _____
   _____

Name: _____ Date: _____

Creating an Antagonist: I've Been Framed!

Most stories include at least one **antagonist**, also known as "the bad guy." The antagonist may be the one who committed the crime, tries to prevent the main character from reaching his or her goal, or is a rival or challenger for a prize.

Draw a person, animal, or object you might use as the antagonist in a short story. Write descriptive words and phrases about the character on the lines.

Save your ideas for an antagonist to use in a future story.

Name: _____ Date: _____

Inanimate Objects as Characters: The Walls Have Ears

Inanimate objects, like a talking teapot, a dancing flower, or a robot, can be main characters in stories.

1. List five stories or movies that have inanimate objects as main characters.

   _____   _____

   _____   _____

   _____

2. Write a short story on your own paper using one of these objects as the main character.

   ➡ a sleepy flower that didn't want to wake up in spring

   ➡ a grumpy rock that didn't like to get wet

   ➡ a robot that thought it was alive

   ➡ a pair of earrings that whispers advice to the wearer

   ➡ a cloud that likes to rain on people having picnics

   ➡ a pair of running shoes that nags its owner about exercise

   ➡ a fork that gives advice about nutrition and table manners

   ➡ a bed that talks to someone while he or she sleeps

   ➡ an old angry tree that doesn't like birds

   ➡ a guitar that allows its owner to play only country-western music

   ➡ a stuffed animal looking for a new home

   ➡ a wall that changes colors and textures

   ➡ an airplane that is afraid of heights

   ➡ a nutcracker that comes to life only on Christmas Eve

3. Proofread, revise, and edit your story. Add a title and hand-drawn illustrations or clip art to the final version.

Name: _____ Date: _____

Punctuating Dialogue: It's Not Fair!

Characters talk to each other in stories. The words they say are called **dialogue**.

Directions: Read the punctuation guidelines for dialogue below. Then underline the dialogue in each sentence.

➡ **Enclose the exact words of a speaker in quotation marks.**

1. "Christmas won't be Christmas without any presents," grumbled Jo, lying on the rug.

➡ **Use exclamation marks inside the quotation marks.**

2. "It's so dreadful to be poor!" sighed Meg, looking down at her old dress.

➡ **Begin a new paragraph each time a different person speaks.**

3. "I don't think it's fair for some girls to have lots of pretty things, and other girls nothing at all," added little Amy, with an injured sniff.

➡ **Use a comma at the end of the quotation, before the quotation marks if the quotation is not the end of the sentence.**

4. "We've got Father and Mother and each other," said Beth contentedly, from her corner.

➡ **Use a comma before the quotation marks if the first part of the sentence is not part of the words of the speaker.**

5. The four young faces upon which the firelight shone brightened at the cheerful words, but darkened again as Jo said sadly, "We haven't got Father, and shall not have him for a long time."

➡ **Use end punctuation inside the quotation marks when a quote ends in a complete sentence.**

6. Nobody spoke for a minute; then Meg said in an altered tone, "You know the reason Mother proposed not having any presents this Christmas was because it's going to be a hard winter for everyone, and she thinks we ought not to spend money for pleasures when our men are suffering so in the army."

From *Little Women* by Louisa May Alcott

Name: _____ Date: _____

Writing and Punctuating Dialogue: Tom Paints a Fence

Dialogue in a story should sound natural—the way people really speak. The words they use and what they say should match the type of characters you want to portray. A conversation between a knight and a dragon would be different from a discussion between two frightened mice.

Directions: Finish the sentences. Add quotation marks, commas, and end punctuation to this dialogue.

1. What 'cha doing Tom asked Henry as he shuffled his bare feet in the dirt.

2. Tom studied the fence before answering Well, you see, Henry, I'm creating a work of art

3. Looks to me like you're painting a fence, Tom _____ Henry.

4. No, _____ Tom. Painting a fence would be work and everyone knows how I feel about work.

5. Is painting a fence a game Can I play Henry _____ eagerly.

6. Oh no! _____ Tom with a wink at his brother.

7. I'll give you my dead toad if you let me paint a while _____ Henry. Please

8. Tom thought a while, then shook his head I reckon Aunt Polly wouldn't allow it. She's mighty particular

Continue writing dialogue between Tom and Henry. Use your own paper if you need more room.

_____

_____

_____

_____

_____

Name: _____ Date: _____

Describing Settings: Sledding Across Frozen Tundra

When and where a story takes place is called the **setting**. Part of writing a story involves describing the setting so well that readers know exactly how it looks, feels, sounds, and smells.

Story settings can be ...

➡ in the past, present, or future;

➡ real places like an apartment building in New York City, a farm in Wisconsin, or a desert in New Mexico;

➡ imaginary places like a magical forest, a land where trees walk and talk, or a school for wizards;

➡ real places that no one has ever visited, such as Pluto, the Sun, or the center of the earth.

Use words and phrases to describe these two scenes.

Name: _____   Date: _____

The Plot Thickens: Elements of a Plot

All good stories need an **interesting plot**—the main idea supported by details about what the characters do, the problems they face, and what happens as a result.

Plots often involve ...

➡ solving personal problems;

➡ overcoming physical obstacles;

➡ undertaking long journeys;

➡ discovering lost or hidden treasures;

➡ accomplishing difficult tasks; or

➡ finding answers.

Answer these questions about the plot of the last book or story you read.

1. What problem did the main character face? _____

    _____

2. How did he or she solve the problem? _____

    _____

3. What physical obstacle did the main character overcome? _____

    _____

4. How did he or she do that? _____

    _____

5. What type of journey was involved?_____

    _____

6. Was the main character searching for anything? If so, what?_____

    _____

7. What difficult task did the main character accomplish?_____

    _____

8. What question did the main character answer? _____

    _____

9. How did the main character change? _____

    _____

Name: _____ Date: _____

Plot Summaries: Good Plots, Dull Plots

A good **plot** encourages readers to continue reading to find out what happens.

1. Draw an asterisk (*) in front of each plot that you think would be interesting.

   _____ After sparing the life of a mouse, a lion is saved by the mouse from being captured.

   _____ A girl went to a mall, bought some clothes, and went home.

   _____ A brave dog saves a young boy from a burning house.

   _____ A pirate searches for buried treasure, but finds something more important.

   _____ A boy and girl overcome many differences to become good friends.

   _____ Space travelers encounter vegetarian inhabitants of a planet where the weather is always perfect.

   _____ A teenager must accomplish three difficult tasks to find happiness.

   _____ A family stranded on a deserted island invents 74 recipes for coconuts.

   _____ A time-traveler journeys to the past and finds herself in the midst of a Civil War battle.

2. Select one of the plot summaries you didn't think would be interesting, and explain why.

   _____

   _____

3. Write three ideas for interesting plots you could use.

   _____

   _____

   _____

   _____

   _____

   _____

4. Write a story on your own paper, using any plot idea from this page. Begin with an interesting opening. Include a description of a main character and the setting in your story. Feel free to go back and review your ideas for characters and settings.

5. Proofread, edit, revise, and rewrite your story.

Name: _____ Date: _____

Sequencing Events: What Happened Next?

Stories usually relate **events in the order in which they occurred**.

1. Complete the sequence of events for the story of "Goldilocks and the Three Bears."

   A. Goldilocks discovered the home of the three bears while walking in the woods.

   B. She went inside and tasted their porridge.

   C. _____
      _____

   D. _____
      _____

   E. _____
      _____

   F. _____
      _____

When you write, listing major events you plan to include can help you organize your story.

An explorer traveling through a deep, dense rain forest in South America discovers a large, heavy chest fastened with chains and a large, sturdy lock. The chest is too heavy to lift. The explorer really wants to open the chest, but has no tools. If he/she leaves, it may be impossible to find the chest again.

2. On your own paper, begin at the point where the explorer has discovered the chest. List the major events that could take place in a story about what the explorer did.

3. When you finish your list, go back and number the events in order.

Rewriting a Conclusion: Change the Ending

The **conclusion** of the story tells what happens at the end. Not all stories end with the words "and they lived happily ever after." O. Henry was a famous author who wrote stories with unexpected endings.

A conclusion could be about what happened when the leprechaun finally reached the end of the rainbow after a long, difficult journey.

At the end of most stories, the main character usually changes in some way. Perhaps the young man found happiness not by marrying the princess but by becoming interested in saving dragons from extinction.

By changing a well-known story, you can create an entirely different ending.

1. Select one of these ideas or use one of your own to create a new ending to a familiar story.

    ➡ Cinderella did not leave the ball by midnight, and her dress turned back into rags in front of everyone.

    ➡ The big, bad wolf succeeded in blowing down all three of the little pigs' houses.

    ➡ When the princess kissed the frog, she turned into a frog too.

    ➡ Snow White did not eat the poisoned apple.

    ➡ Aladdin never found a magic lamp.

    ➡ Dorothy decided to continue living in Oz.

    ➡ Hansel and Gretel made friends with the witch and visited her often in the gingerbread house.

2. Write your story on your own paper. Begin at the part in the story where you want to make the change, and continue from there.

3. Share your new ending with a friend or family member.

Details Are Important: Adding Meaningful Details—Part 1

When writing a story, include important **details**. One way to do that is to ask yourself questions about each major event in the story.

First major event:
Two people drove along a lonely highway through the desert.

You might ask these questions:

- ➡ Why were they driving there?
- ➡ Where were they going?
- ➡ What were their names?
- ➡ How old were they?
- ➡ What kind of car were they driving?
- ➡ What color was their car?
- ➡ What time of day was it?
- ➡ What time of year was it?
- ➡ What did the desert look like?
- ➡ Were they retired?
- ➡ Were they on their honeymoon?
- ➡ Which person was driving?
- ➡ Were they two men? Two women? A man and a woman?
- ➡ How did they feel?
- ➡ Were they hot, tired, and grumpy? Relaxed and happy?

As you think about the answers to these questions, you can decide which details are important for the reader. Remember, not all details are important. Too many details can make a story long and boring.

As you write, ask yourself:

- ➡ Does the reader need more information?
- ➡ Would adding details make the story more interesting?

On your own paper, write an interesting opening paragraph for this story. Include details you think are important.

Save your paragraph, and continue with the activity on the next page.

Name: _____ Date: _____

Details Are Important: Adding Meaningful Details—Part 2

Second major event:

Suddenly, the driver slammed on the brakes, pulled over to the side of the road, and backed up 100 feet.

To add more details, you could ask yourself:
- ➡ Would this be a good place to include dialogue?
- ➡ What did the passenger say?

List two more questions you could ask yourself about this part of the story to provide more details.

_____

_____

Third major event:

The driver hurried to the center of the road, where a large tortoise was slowly shuffling across. The driver carried the tortoise across the road and set it down among some tumbleweeds.

List questions about this part of the story.

_____

_____

_____

_____

Fourth major event:

The tortoise thanked the driver and offered to grant three wishes to repay this kindness.

What questions could you answer to provide more details about this part of the story?

_____

_____

_____

_____

Save this page. Continue with the activity on the next page.

Name: _____ Date: _____

Details Are Important: Adding Meaningful Details—Part 3

Add questions you could answer to provide details about each of these events.

Fifth major event:

The driver made the first wish.

_____

_____

_____

_____

Sixth major event:

The passenger made the second wish.

_____

_____

_____

_____

Seventh major event:

One person made the third wish.

_____

_____

_____

_____

Go back and read your opening paragraph. Now that you know the rest of the events in the story, revise and edit your beginning.

Continue writing the story on your own paper. The list of major events will be the plot for your story. Your questions will help you add important details. The ending of the story is entirely up to you! Don't forget to add a title. Good luck, and have fun writing!

Name: _____ Date: _____

Abstract Ideas: What Does Freedom Mean to You?

You can describe an **abstract idea** by defining it and giving examples.

Some abstract ideas you could write about are:

love
charity
goodness
cooperation

respect
freedom
morality
consideration

bravery
honesty
patriotism
thoughtfulness

loyalty
kindness
friendship

1. Select one of the ideas listed or another abstract idea that is important to you. Write words and phrases to answer these questions.

    A. What does this idea mean to you?_____

    _____

    B. Why is it important? _____

    _____

    C. What makes a person honest or kind or brave or whatever characteristic you have chosen?

    _____

    _____

    D. What did you or someone else do that showed an example of this trait?

    _____

    _____

2. On your own paper, write about a character trait and what it means to you. Include your definition and an example of that trait.

3. Proofread, edit, and revise your work before rewriting.

Name: _____ Date: _____

Writing Myths: Why the Sky Is Blue

People in every culture tell myths, some of which have been handed down for thousands of years. Myths often have three purposes: to explain, to instruct, and to entertain.

Myths are stories about gods, heroes, animals, or memorable events. Some myths provide nonscientific explanations for natural events, like why we have winter, why the sky is blue, or how the world began. The setting for many myths involves a time before the world as we know it came to be.

Not all myths are thousands of years old. Rudyard Kipling wrote a book called *Just So Stories* in 1903, about a time long ago when the world was new, before there were people. Then, the animals could talk. Many looked very different from the way they do today. Elephant had a short trunk. Bear's tail was long and fluffy. Rhinoceroses didn't have wrinkled skin.

Read several myths, ancient or modern, from any culture. You can find collections of myths at the library and on the Internet.

1. Write a brief summary of one myth you read.

   _____

   _____

   _____

   _____

Myths could explain ...

- ➡ why the sky is blue.
- ➡ why we have night and day.
- ➡ how the world began.
- ➡ why giraffes have long necks.
- ➡ why it is hotter in summer than winter.

- ➡ why zebras have stripes.
- ➡ why giant redwood trees grow so large.
- ➡ how mountains were born.
- ➡ why roses have thorns.
- ➡ how the sun moves across the sky.

2. Write two other natural events that could be explained by a myth.

   _____

   _____

   _____

3. On your own paper, use one of the ideas above, or one of your own, to write a myth explaining any natural event.

4. Proofread, edit, and revise your myth. Add a title, and draw illustrations or add clip art to the final copy.

Name: _____ Date: _____

Round Robins and Brainstorming

A **round robin** is a story written by several people who take turns adding to the story.

To create a "round robin":

➡ Begin by brainstorming for story ideas. Ask each member of the group to contribute suggestions.

➡ The first person writes an interesting sentence to begin the story and reads it out loud to the group.

➡ The second person adds a sentence or two and reads it out loud.

➡ People in the group continue taking turns adding sentences until the story is complete.

1. Write ideas for a main character.

2. Include ideas for the setting (time and place).

3. Jot down ideas for a plot.

4. If you like your group story, work together to polish it. Proofread, edit, and revise your story. Decide on a title.

5. One member of the group can type the story on the computer and make copies for the others.

6. If you don't like your story, start over and try again.

Name: _____ Date: _____

Time To Review: Fiction

Use the words in the box to complete the activity below. Write the correct term on the line under each statement.

1. Stories that portray the humorous adventures of super characters

    _____

2. Stories with plots that involve a crime or puzzling event that the main character solves

    _____

3. Stories that often take place in magical places and include characters like giants, elves, wizards, and trolls

    _____

4. When and where a story takes place

    _____

| thesaurus |
| fantasies |
| tall tales |
| plot |
| setting |
| antagonist |
| dialogue |
| science fiction |
| mysteries |
| myths |
| fables |

5. A story character who commits a crime or tries to prevent the main character from reaching a goal or winning a prize

    _____

6. Stories that teach a lesson _____

7. Stories about gods, heroes, animals, or events written to explain natural events like the seasons

    _____

8. A book that provides synonyms _____

9. The words said by a character in a story _____

10. The main idea of a story that is supported by details about what the characters do, the problems they face, and what happens as a result

    _____

11. Stories that include scientific knowledge and speculation as a major part of the plot, setting, or theme

    _____

Name: _____ Date: _____

What Is Poetry?

Poetry is more than a collection of words divided into lines and stanzas.

- ❀ Poems come in many sizes and shapes.

- ❀ Some are long narratives (stories).

- ❀ Some poems use humor or puns to entertain the reader.

- ❀ Poets use words, sounds, and imagery to paint word pictures.

- ❀ Poetry can describe scenes in nature.

- ❀ Poetry can express the poet's feelings and emotions.

- ❀ Some poems rhyme, and some don't.

Poetry is a way to communicate experiences, emotions, ideas, and thoughts using rhyme, rhythm, sound patterns, and imagery.

1. List three poems you enjoy. _____

_____

When you write a paragraph, you learn how important it is to begin with an interesting topic sentence. The first line of a poem is important as well.

2. Read these opening lines written by Edgar Allan Poe.

    A. Once upon a midnight dreary, as I pondered, weak and weary,

    B. At midnight in the month of June,

    C. The happiest day—the happiest hour

    D. Lo! 'tis a gala night,

    E. By a route obscure and lonely,

    Which opening line do you like best? _____ Why? _____

    _____

3. Write an opening line for a poem about night. _____

_____

_____

Name: _____ Date: _____

Rhyme Time: Couplets

Many poems use end **rhymes**.

Example: Hey, diddle, diddle,
                The cat and the fiddle,
                The cow jumped over the moon.
                The little dog laughed to see such sport
                And the dish ran away with the spoon.

Rhymes can be one-syllable words. Examples of one-syllable words that rhyme with *moon* and *spoon* are *boon, dune, June, loon, noon, rune, soon,* and *tune.*

Rhyming words can also be more than one syllable, as long as the last syllable rhymes. Other words that rhyme with *moon* and *spoon* are *baboon, balloon, lagoon,* and *typhoon.*

Directions: For each word, write ten or more words that rhyme. Then write a two-line poem using end rhyme. Two lines that rhyme are called a **couplet**.

Words that rhyme with *trees*: _____

_____

_____

Your poem: _____

_____

Words that rhyme with *way*: _____

_____

_____

Your poem: _____

_____

Words that rhyme with *clock*: _____

_____

_____

Your poem: _____

_____

Name: _____ Date: _____

Looking Closely at a Poem: Robert Frost

Stopping By Woods on a Snowy Evening
By Robert Frost

Whose woods these are I think I know.
His house is in the village though:
He will not see me stopping here
To watch his woods fill up with snow.

My little horse must think it queer
To stop without a farmhouse near
Between the woods and frozen lake
The darkest evening of the year.

He gives his harness bells a shake
To ask if there is some mistake.
The only other sound's the sweep
Of easy wind and downy flake.

The woods are lovely, dark and deep.
But I have promises to keep.
And miles to go before I sleep.
And miles to go before I sleep.

Read "Stopping By Woods on a Snowy Evening" several times before answering the questions.

1. What is the mood of this poem? (How does it make you feel?) _____

_____

_____

2. When and where does the action occur? _____

_____

3. Study the rhyme scheme. How is the last stanza different? _____

_____

_____

4. Why do you think Robert Frost used repetition for the last two lines? _____

_____

_____

5. Did you enjoy this poem? Why or why not? _____

_____

_____

Name: _____   Date: _____

Descriptive Adjectives

When poets write **descriptive poetry**, they use adjectives and descriptive phrases to paint word pictures.

For each illustration, write on the lines words and phrases that describe or are related to the topic.

Name: _____ Date: _____

Expressing an Idea: I Believe

Many poems are written to **express ideas**. Any subject you feel strongly about can be the topic for a poem.

Begin with a statement of belief.

❀ I believe honesty is the basis for trust.

❀ I believe everyone has the right to freedom from fear.

❀ I believe prejudice in any form is wrong.

1. Write statements of belief on subjects about which you have strong feelings.

   I believe _____

   I believe _____

   I believe _____

   I believe _____

   I believe _____

2. Select one of your statements as a topic for a poem. Write one word that summarizes the idea.

   _____

3. Write three synonyms for that word. (Synonyms are words that mean the same, or nearly the same, thing.)

   _____   _____   _____

4. Write three antonyms for that word. (Antonyms are words that have opposite meanings.)

   _____   _____   _____

5. Expand on your topic by writing words and phrases related to the topic.

   _____

   _____

   _____

   _____

6. Use your ideas to write a poem about your topic. Add a title. Write your finished poem on fancy paper.

Name: _____ Date: _____

Punctuating Poetry: End Punctuation and Commas

Before writing the final version of your poems, you must proofread them, always correcting punctuation errors. Poetry is punctuated similarly to prose.

Use end punctuation (periods, question marks, or exclamation points) after all complete sentences.

1. Add end punctuation where it is needed in this limerick.

> I went to the animal fair
> The lions and tigers were there
> An old baboon
> By the light of the moon
> Was combing his long red hair
>
> A monkey got in a funk
> He tripped on the elephant's trunk
> The elephant sneezed
> And fell to his knees
> Well, that was the end of the monk

If poems contain phrases that are not complete sentences, end punctuation is not used. Commas can be used at the end of each line, except when the thought on one line continues to the next.

2. Add end punctuation and commas to these poems.

Thunderstorm

> Bolts of lightning
> Ripping apart the sky
> Shattering the night
> Flashing off and on
> Like a demented strobe light

Lost and Found

> Where do thoughts go when you lose them
> Do they vanish forever
> If you find a lost thought
> Can you pretend it followed you home
> And claim it for your own

Name: _____ Date: _____

Punctuating Poetry: End Punctuation and Commas (cont.)

Use **commas** to separate three or more nouns in a series.

> *Example:* Dolphins, sharks, manta rays, and seahorses swam together in the aquarium.

Use **commas** to separate two or more adjectives when they describe a noun.

> *Example:* The big, black bug bit the busy, big, brown bear.

1. Add commas and end punctuation to this poem.

A Rainbow Garden

Red blue purple orange and yellow flowers
Shout to passersby with their brightly colored blooms
Her garden was a rainbow of
Tulips roses daisies and lilies
Free for all to enjoy

2. Write a noun. _____

3. Write three adjectives to describe the noun.

_____   _____   _____

4. Write three words ending in *-ing* related to the noun.

_____   _____   _____

5. Write another noun that is a synonym for the first one.

_____

6. You have just written a poem! Now go back and add punctuation and a title.

Name: _____   Date: _____

Alliteration: Polly Porter Packed Purple Pumpkins

Alliteration is the repetition of a letter sound at the beginning or in the middle of words. Alliteration in poetry can be used to create a mood or as a way to have fun with words.

1. Read the alliterative examples out loud. Try to keep your tongue from getting tangled!

Polly Porter packed a peck of purple pumpkins.
A peck of purple pumpkins Polly Porter packed.
If Polly Porter packed a peck of purple pumpkins,
How many purple pumpkins did Polly Porter pack?

Brian Borden bought a barrel of bitter butter-beets.
A barrel of bitter butter-beets Brian Borden bought.
If Brian Borden bought a barrel of bitter butter-beets,
How many bitter-butter beets did Brian Borden buy?

2. Write ideas for alliteration poems. Use a different letter sound for each line.

A Two-Word Name	An Action	An Adjective	An Item
_____	_____	_____	_____
_____	_____	_____	_____
_____	_____	_____	_____
_____	_____	_____	_____

3. Use one of your ideas to write a four-line alliterative poem using the same format as the examples.

_____

_____

_____

_____

Read your poem out loud to a friend.

Name: _____ Date: _____

Capitalization Counts

The same rules for **capitalization** apply to prose and poetry. When you proofread your writing, keep these capitalization rules in mind.

Always capitalize ...

✿ the word *I*.

✿ the first word in each line of poetry.

✿ the first word in each sentence.

✿ names of specific people, places, and things.

Examples: Bart Starr, White House, the Constitution

1. Write two examples of specific people:

_____   _____

2. Write two examples of specific places:

_____   _____

3. Write two examples of specific things:

_____   _____

✿ the days of the week and months of the year

✿ people's titles when used with their names

Examples: Dr. Jones, President Lincoln

4. Write two more examples: _____   _____

✿ the names of cities, states, countries

Examples: Paris, France; Boston, Massachusetts

5. Write two more examples: _____   _____

✿ the important words in titles of books, stories, movies, songs, plays, poems, etc.

Example: Snow White and the Seven Dwarfs

6. Write another example*:* _____

✿ the names of lakes, mountains, and oceans

Examples: Rocky Mountains, Atlantic Ocean

7. Write two more examples: _____   _____

Name: _____ Date: _____

Replace Dull Words: Synonyms

By using more interesting words or **synonyms**, writers paint a clearer word picture. A synonym is a word that means the same or nearly the same thing as another word. Instead of the word *looked*, you could use *searched, gazed, glanced, stared, peeked, scanned,* or *gawked*.

All of these words are similar to *looked*, but have more specialized meanings and paint a clearer word picture.

When you need to find interesting words to replace dull ones, use a thesaurus.

1. Use a thesaurus to find three or more interesting words to replace the words listed.

   went: _____ _____ _____

   said: _____ _____ _____

   ran: _____ _____ _____

   give: _____ _____ _____

2. Replace the underlined words in the poem with more interesting ones. You may also change any other words. Rewrite the poem.

   A Bad Hair Day

   She <u>looks</u> in the mirror
   And frowns
   At the sleep tangles
   That <u>came</u> in the night.
   She <u>knows</u> it <u>will be</u>
   A bad hair day.

_____

_____

_____

_____

_____

_____

_____

Name: _____ Date: _____

Writing Haiku

Haiku is a formal type of poetry with a very specific pattern:
- ❀   Each poem is only three lines long.
- ❀   The first and third lines contain exactly five syllables.
- ❀   The second line contains exactly seven syllables.

1. Count the syllables and write the number on the blanks by each line.

Fog

_____   Silent fog creeping

_____   Out of the October night

_____   Smothering the world

Haiku poems paint word pictures about topics that are often related to nature or to one of the seasons. Writers use haiku to express strong feelings about a topic.

2. To write haiku, first decide on a season and/or something in nature related to that season. You can use your own ideas or one from this list below.

- ❀   a winter blizzard
- ❀   a hot, steamy rain forest
- ❀   a forest on a hot summer night
- ❀   the stillness after a snowstorm
- ❀   a cold, lonely bird shivering in the winter
- ❀   waves crashing on the shore on a bleak spring day
- ❀   a spring thunderstorm
- ❀   mountains covered with snow
- ❀   the ocean on a still summer day
- ❀   a tree without leaves on a windy fall day

3. List three possible topics for your haiku poem.

_____

_____

_____

Since haiku uses so few words, poets know how important it is to use exactly the right words. A thesaurus is very helpful when writing haiku.

3. Write each of your topics on your own paper. Then add related words and phrases. Use interesting words to paint a word picture or to create a feeling.

4. Polish your haiku poems. Count the number of syllables in each line. Write the final version on fancy paper. Illustration is optional.

Name: _____ Date: _____

Sing Me a Poem: Rhyme and Repetition

Many of the songs you learned when you were young are actually simple **rhyming poems** set to music.

Row, Row, Row Your Boat

Row, row, row your boat
Gently down the stream
Merrily, merrily, merrily, merrily
Life is but a dream.

A common feature in many children's songs is the repetition of a word or phrase. Examples include "London Bridge," "The Farmer in the Dell," "Head, Shoulders, Knees, and Toes," and "The Wheels on the Bus."

1. List other songs that use rhyme and/or repetition.

    _____

    _____

    _____

    _____

    _____

Some songs contain nonsense words or sounds, like hickory, dickory, dock or E–I–E–I–O.

2. List other songs that use nonsense words or sounds.

    _____

    _____

    _____

    _____

You can create your own song poems by writing new words to familiar melodies.

4. Start with a familiar song. Then begin changing the words. Instead of "row, row, row your boat," you could try "drive, drive, drive your van;" "fly, fly, fly your plane;" or "ride, ride, ride your bike."

5. When your song poem is finished, sing it with a friend.

Name: _____ Date: _____

Sensory Poems: Use Your Senses

Sensory poems use words related to sight, sound, smell, taste, and touch to provide specific images for the reader.

Fresh-Baked Bread

I watch hungrily as my mother opens the oven
To check the progress of the bread.
My eyes devour the lightly browned crust.
The mouth-watering aroma drifts across the kitchen.
The delicious fragrance sneaks silently
Past my nose into my brain.
My tongue searches for a taste.
My empty stomach shouts,
"Eat! Eat! Eat!"
Mother says, "A few more minutes."

1. Which senses does the writer include? _____

   _____

   _____

2. A successful sensory poem allows the reader to become a part of the experience. Do you think "Fresh-Baked Bread" is a successful sensory poem?

   _____

   Why or why not? _____

   _____

   _____

3. Write other words and phrases about the sight, smell, taste, or feel of fresh, hot bread.

   _____

   _____

   _____

   _____

   _____

   _____

Name: _____ Date: _____

Use Your Senses: Sensory Poems (cont.)

1. Write sensory words and phrases to describe each item.

    the taste of ice cream on a hot summer day _____

    _____

    the sounds of early morning _____

    _____

    the sight of waves crashing on a beach _____

    _____

    the smell of fresh, hot popcorn _____

    _____

    the feel of wind on a blustery day _____

    _____

2. Use sensory words and phrases to describe a crowded, sandy beach on a hot summer day.

    sights: _____

    _____

    sounds: _____

    _____

    tastes: _____

    _____

    smells: _____

    _____

    touch: _____

    _____

3. Use sensory words and phrases to describe a houseful of relatives enjoying a Thanksgiving dinner with all the trimmings.

    sights: _____

    sounds: _____

    tastes: _____

    smells: _____

    touch: _____

4. On your own paper, write a sensory poem. Provide the reader with descriptions that include at least three senses.

Name: _____ Date: _____

Nonsense Poems: Limericks

Limericks are five-line poems that use rhythm and rhyme. Lines 1, 2, and 5 are longer and end in rhyming words. Lines 3 and 4 rhyme with each other and are shorter than the other lines.

Example 1:   There once was a seventh-grade lad
Whose poems were exceedingly bad.
The only thing worse
Than his terrible verse
Were the ones that he learned from his dad.

Example 2:   There once was a girl called Diana
Whose favorite food was banana.
She ate them at meals
And saved all the peels
To build a big house in Montana.

1. In *Example 1*, what three words are used as end rhymes for lines one, two, and five?

   _____

   What two words are used as end rhymes for lines three and four?

   _____

   The number of syllables in each line determines the rhythm of the poem. Lines one, two, and five should all contain about the same number of syllables. Lines three and four should contain about the same number of syllables, but less than the other lines.

2. In *Example 2*, how many syllables are in each line?

   Line 1 _____   Line 2 _____   Line 3 _____

   Line 4 _____   Line 5 _____

3. Write two limericks on your own paper. You may need to revise several times before you finish. Before you write the final version, check the rhyme scheme and the number of syllables in each line.

   For more examples of limericks, check out *Nonsense Poems* by Edward Lear and *Pigericks* by Arnold Lobel.

   Hold a limerick-writing contest with your group, and vote for the funniest poem.

Name: _____ Date: _____

Narrative Poems: Poems Can Tell Stories

A **narrative poem** tells a story. Narratives can be serious poems about famous events or people. They can tell about actual events or be totally fictional. Some narratives tell humorous stories.

Poem	Author
"Paul Revere's Ride"	Henry Wadsworth Longfellow
"John Brown's Body"	Stephen Vincent Benét
"Lincoln"	Nancy Byrd Turner
"A Visit from St. Nicholas"	Clement Moore
"The Raggedy Man"	James Whitcomb Riley
"Robinson Crusoe's Story"	Charles E. Carryl
"The Pied Piper of Hamelin"	Robert Browning
"Jabberwocky"	Lewis Carroll
"Casey at the Bat"	Ernest Lawrence Thayer
"The Owl and the Pussycat"	Edward Lear

Read a narrative poem. You'll find many examples at your library or on the Internet.

1. What was the title? _____

2. Who wrote the poem? _____

3. Was the narrative serious or humorous? _____

4. Was the story about a real person or event? _____

5. Who was the main character? _____

6. When and where did the story take place? _____

   _____

7. Write a summary of the poem. _____

   _____

   _____

   _____

   _____

8. Did you like the poem? Why or why not? _____

   _____

   _____

Name: _____ Date: _____

Narrative Poems: Write a Story Poem

A **narrative poem** tells a story. Some narratives are quite long, like "The Iliad" and "The Odyssey" written by Homer. Narrative poems can also be short.

The first example is based on an Aesop's fable: "The Dog and the Shadow." The second example summarizes the story of "Goldilocks and the Three Bears."

The Greedy Dog

There once was a dog filled with greed
Who wanted much more than he'd need.
When he saw his reflection
Upon further inspection
He ended with nothing, indeed.

Goldilocks

Goldilocks visited the three famous bears
She ate all their food and she sat on their chairs.
When she was sleepy, she climbed into the bed.
When the bears returned home, Goldilocks fled.

Some narrative poems use end-rhymes like the two examples, but rhyme is not necessary.

A narrative poem could summarize a well-known story or tell a new story. It could be based on a current news event or something that actually happened to you.

1. List ideas for a narrative poem you might write.

    _____

    _____

    _____

    _____

2. Select the story you want to tell. Who is the main character? _____

3. When and where does the story take place? _____

    _____

4. Write a short summary of the plot and conclusion.

    _____

    _____

    _____

    _____

5. Write your narrative poem on your own paper. Edit, proofread, revise, and polish your poem. Add a title. You can draw your own illustrations or use computer clip art.

Name: _____ Date: _____

Time to Review: Poetry

Use the words in the box to help you identify the terms related to poetry described below.

1. Figures of speech that compare two unlike objects or
   ideas without using the words *like* or *as*

   _____

2. Poems that use words related to sight, sound, smell,
   taste, and touch to provide specific images

   _____

3. Wrote "Stopping By Woods on a Snowy Evening"

   _____

4. Two lines that rhyme _____

5. Five-line humorous poems that rhyme

   _____

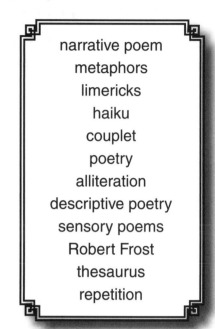

narrative poem
metaphors
limericks
haiku
couplet
poetry
alliteration
descriptive poetry
sensory poems
Robert Frost
thesaurus
repetition

6. Repetition of a letter sound at the beginning or in the middle of words used to create a
   mood or for humor _____

7. A way to communicate experiences, emotions, ideas, and thoughts using rhyme, rhythm,
   sound patterns, and imagery _____

8. A formal type of poetry containing three lines, often written about nature and/or a season

   _____

9. A poem that tells a story _____

10. Poetry that uses adjectives and descriptive phrases to paint word pictures

    _____

11. A book that lists synonyms for words _____

12. Repeating something over and over _____

Name: _____ Date: _____

Nonfiction Writing: Why Write Reports?

A **report** is a summary of material available on a given subject. Report writing involves using information already known to present facts about a topic in an interesting and exciting way.

People in many businesses and professions write reports. They need to be able to present information in a concise, logical manner that is readable and accurate. Someone has to write those reports. That someone may be you someday.

Contractors may write daily reports of what happened on a job site, or they may have to write accident reports. They would read reports on new construction materials or techniques.

Administrative assistants might write reports summarizing problems in an office or difficulties with equipment. They might read reports on new types of office equipment available.

A personnel manager would find a report about wages and hiring practices in the community useful.

Doctors read reports about new treatments, medications, tests, technology, and equipment available to keep up with changes in their field.

For each occupation, describe a type of report that person might write and a type of report that person might find helpful to read.

	Write	**Read**
A plant supervisor	_____	_____
A scientist	_____	_____
A mechanic	_____	_____
A lawyer	_____	_____
A dentist	_____	_____
A teacher	_____	_____
An author	_____	_____

Name: _____ Date: _____

Choosing a Topic: A Piece of Cake

Completing a report is like eating a piece of cake. Before you can eat the cake, many other tasks must be completed.

Someone must raise the chickens and cows, gather the eggs, and milk the cows. The flour, sugar, and other ingredients must also be produced and prepared for use. A baker needs to find a recipe, gather ingredients, and finally bake the cake.

You don't have to raise the chickens, milk the cows, or raise the wheat before you write a report, but you do need to complete many other tasks.

The first step in writing a report is choosing the topic and focusing on one aspect of that topic.

Even if the topic is assigned, writers have some leeway in how to present the material. For example, if ten bakers were asked to make chocolate cakes, you might have ten completely different shapes and types of chocolate cake.

If you were asked to write a report on the United States, the topic would be too broad to cover in a report. You would need to **focus** on one aspect of the topic.

Perhaps you would like to write about the Civil War. Is that topic still too broad? Absolutely!

You could decide to narrow the topic even more:

- The causes of the Civil War
- Women soldiers in the Civil War
- The effects of the Civil War on the South
- General Grant's role in the Civil War
- The final battle of the Civil War

1. Why would it be difficult to write about a very large topic like the United States in a school report?

   _____

   _____

   _____

2. List one other idea about the Civil War that might be a good topic for a report.

   _____

   _____

   _____

Name: _____ Date: _____

Topics: Three Things to Keep in Mind

When you focus on a topic for a report, try to keep **three things** in mind:

A. Is the topic focused enough to be manageable?

Topic: A planet in our solar system
Focus: The development of life on Earth

1. Do you think this topic is focused enough to be manageable? Why or why not?

_____

_____

B. Is the topic too focused? Will you be able to find enough information for your report?

Topic: Sports
Focus: The type of material used to make covers for baseballs.

2. Do you think this topic is too focused? Why or why not?

_____

_____

C. Does the topic interest you?

Topic: Dinosaurs
Focus: Tyrannosaurs in North America

3. Does the topic interest you?

_____

_____

If your goal is to write a report on birds, there are many options available for your topic selection. Select one that interests you.

If you are interested in one particular type of bird or one area of bird behavior, the decision may be easy. If not, you may need to do some research before you decide on your final topic.

To narrow a topic and find one of interest to you, you could begin by paging through general reference books about birds. You could talk to someone who raises birds.

4. What else could you do to narrow the topic and find one that interests you?

_____

_____

_____

_____

Name: _____ Date: _____

Getting Focused

To write a report about a sport when you don't have a particular favorite, you could begin by making a list of sports.

1. Make a list of sports that could be topics for a report.

    _____

    _____

After you select one sport, narrow the topic. Would you like to write about the history of that sport? The rules? Famous players?

2. What could be the focus for a report on sports that would interest you?

    _____

    _____

If you are still having trouble deciding on a topic, try brainstorming, alone or with a small group. Toss ideas around with friends and family members.

General topic: Mammals
More specific topic: Cats
Focused topic: Jaguars

Fill in the blanks. Use the example at right.

General topic: Dinosaurs

More specific topic: _____

Focused topic: _____

General topic: Our solar system

More specific topic: _____

Focused topic: _____

General topic: Music

More specific topic: _____

Focused topic: _____

General topic: Computer software

More specific topic: _____

Focused topic: _____

Name: _____ Date: _____

Report Topics

1. Circle three topics on the list below that interest you. Then on the lines below, list a specific focus for each topic that you could use for a report.

Air	**Art**	**Asia**	**Birds**	**Boats**	**Camping**
Cars	**Cities**	**Computers**	**Cooking**	**Fall**	**Families**
Fire	**Fish**	**Flowers**	**Food**	**Fossils**	**Games**
Gems	**Germs**	**Hats**	**Hiking**	**History**	**Holidays**
Houses	**Lakes**	**Maps**	**Mars**	**Math**	**Mud**
Paper	**People**	**Pets**	**Plants**	**Rain**	**Rocks**
Safety	**Science**	**Shells**	**Spiders**	**Spies**	**Stars**
Suns	**Toys**	**Trees**	**Weather**	**Weeds**	**Winter**

_____

_____

_____

Time to Decide

2. What is the topic for your report? _____

3. Brainstorm for ideas to narrow the focus of your topic.

_____

_____

_____

4. List ideas you could focus on for a report that would interest you. _____

_____

_____

_____

5. When you decide on the focus for your report, write a sentence stating the main idea.

    Examples:

    My report will compare the two leaders during the Civil War: Abraham Lincoln and Jefferson Davis.

    My report will be about how Rosa Parks helped the cause of civil rights.

    My report will _____

_____

_____

Name: _____ Date: _____

Questions Lead to Answers

Once you have a focus for your report, make a list of questions about your topic. Having specific questions in mind can help you look for specific answers.

For a report on wolves, you could list questions like these:

→ How big are they?
→ What color are they?
→ What do they eat?
→ Where do they live?
→ What is their habitat like?
→ Do they have any natural enemies?
→ Are they endangered?

1. List questions you might ask before writing a report on the origin of baseball.

_____

_____

_____

_____

_____

_____

_____

Use the basic questions of *Who?, What?, When?, Where?, Why?,* and *How?,* but make them specific to your topic.

2. List questions related to your topic. Write each question on your own paper.

As you find answers, you can write the information on the same page as the question. This will help you organize your report when you get to the writing stage.

Sometimes the answer to one question leads to more questions. No problem—you can always add more questions.

3. How can asking questions help you write your report?

_____

_____

_____

_____

Keep Track of Your Sources

A **bibliography** is a list of sources used to write a report. The bibliography is included on the last page of your report.

If you need to include a bibliography with your report, write down the information you'll need as you do your research.

You will need this information for a bibliography:

◆ Authors of books or articles (print or electronic)

◆ Titles of books or articles (print or electronic)

◆ Volume numbers of books, if part of a set

◆ Page numbers of any material quoted in your report

◆ Page numbers of magazine, newspaper, and encyclopedia articles

◆ Date published; for magazine and newspaper articles, include the day, month, and year

◆ Names of publishers of books, magazines, or newspapers

◆ City, state, and/or country where books, magazines, or newspapers were published

◆ Internet addresses of online sources

◆ Names of people you interview and dates of interviews

It's important to keep an ongoing list of books, magazines, newspapers, Internet sites, and other sources as you research your report.

Keep track of your sources by writing the information for each source on a separate note card as you use it. Use letters to code your note cards. The first note card you write can be A, the next one B, etc.

As you write answers to your questions and take notes, use the letter code of the reference source in case you want to go back and check for more details later.

There are many acceptable formats for writing a bibliography. Ask your teacher for samples of the format you should use.

Samples for a Bibliography

Follow the order and punctuation shown in the samples to write your bibliography.

A book:

Author's name (last name first). Title of book (underlined).
Publication location: Publishing company name. Date published.

Example: Casetta, Cindy. <u>My Trip to Pluto</u>. Lunar Base 11: Future Publishing Company. 2274.

An encyclopedia article:

Title of article (enclosed in quotation marks). Name of the encyclopedia (underlined). Author's name, if given. Volume and page numbers of the article: Publication location: Publishing company name. Date published.

Example: "The Truth about Pluto." <u>International Galactic Multidimensional Encyclopedia</u>. Cindy Casetta. Vol. 274, 2–98: Andromeda: Intergalactic Publishing. 2274.

A newspaper or magazine article:

Author's name, if listed (last name first). Title of article (enclosed in quotation marks). Title of publication (underlined). Volume number if listed: Date published: page number(s).

Example: Brown, Dr. Jay C. "Fun with Algebra." <u>Math Weekly</u>. Volume 1: January 1, 2052: 4–17.

A website:

Author's name, if listed (last name first). Title of article, if given (enclosed in quotation marks). Name of website (underlined). Date published. Name of organization (if available). Date accessed. Website address (use < > to set it apart)

Example: Brown, Dr. Jay C. "Statistics are Your Friends." <u>All About Statistics</u>. June 12, 2052. Statistics and You. September 7, 2052. <www.drjaycb/phd_stats.edu>

Footnotes and Endnotes

Footnotes identify material taken directly from other sources. All direct quotations must be noted.

Material taken from other sources is numbered. A footnote with a matching number is placed at the foot (bottom) of the page in your report where the quotation appears.

Endnotes are numbered like footnotes, but are placed at the end of a report.

Footnotes and endnotes are numbered consecutively when they appear in a report.

"The best things in life are worth striving for."[1]

The second quotation would be [2], and so on.

Information to include in footnotes and endnotes:
➜ name of author (first name followed by last name)
➜ title of book (underlined)
➜ title of article (in quotation marks)
➜ name of reference source (underlined)
➜ location of publisher, name of publisher, and date published (in parentheses)
➜ volume number and page number
➜ website address if online source

A book with one author:

Example: Cindy Casetta. My Trip to Pluto, (Lunar Base 11: Future Publishing Company, 2274) 71.

A magazine or newspaper article:

Example: Dr. Jay C. Brown. "Fun with Algebra," Math Weekly, (January 1, 2052) Vol. 1: 17.

An encyclopedia article:

Example: Cindy Casetta. "The Truth about Pluto," International Galactic Multidimensional Encyclopedia, (Andromeda: Intergalactic Publishing, 2274) Vol. 274: 82.

A Website:

Example: Dr. Jay C. Brown. "Statistics are Your Friends." <www.drjaycb/phd_stats.edu> September 7, 2052.

Name: _____ Date: _____

Finding Material at the Library

Having the best tools in the world won't help a builder if he can't find them or doesn't know how to use them. Nor will the best library in the world help you write your report if you don't know how to find and use the tools you need.

Materials in libraries are divided into two groups: fiction and nonfiction. Fiction is arranged in alphabetical order according to the last name of the author.

To find a reference book, begin with the library's computer catalog. Many libraries have online catalogs you can use from your home or school computer. If you don't know the Internet address for your library, call and ask.

To use the computer catalog, type your topic in the subject line and click on the "search" or "go" button. A list of materials on that subject appears on the screen.

Click on an entry for more information about a specific book and where to find it.

1. Look up your topic in the library catalog. Write the titles and numbers of three books you might use for your report.

   _____

   _____

   _____

   Nonfiction material is arranged in a number order called the Dewey Decimal System. In the Dewey Decimal System, all numbers and letters are important.

2. Why would a book numbered 551.7 come before one numbered 551.71?

   _____

   _____

3. Why would a book numbered 337.35M come after one numbered 337.35L?

   _____

   _____

4. Arrange these Dewey Decimal numbers in order from lowest to highest. Number them from 1 to 10, with 1 being the lowest number.

   A. _____ 372.623J2   B. _____ 487.5

   C. _____ 522.91   D. _____ 487.639

   E. _____ 522.199   F. _____ 372.633

   G. _____ 614.901   H. _____ 327.284U1

   I. _____ 522.918   J. _____ 477.614N3

Name: _____ Date: _____

More Tools at the Library

The types of reference materials you will use for your report will depend partly on your topic and partly on what is available. Besides encyclopedias, you'll find other types of reference materials at the library.

An **atlas** provides different types of maps, as well as information about countries, cities, population, time zones, mountains, bodies of water, etc.

1. List the name of one atlas at your library.

    _____

2. Do you plan to use an atlas? Why or why not?

    _____

    _____

Almanacs are often useful because they are published each year, and they contain fairly up-to-date information. You can find statistics about topics like sports, population, religion, national parks, movies, actors, and many other topics in an almanac.

3. List the name of one almanac at your library.

    _____

4. Will you use an almanac? Why or why not?

    _____

    _____

Magazine and newspaper articles are another good source for current information on a topic. Your librarian can help you search for articles on your topic.

5. Will you use magazine or newspaper articles? Why or why not?

    _____

    _____

6. Why do you think it is important to use the most up-to-date sources available, even if your topic involves a person or event from long ago?

    _____

    _____

As you search for answers, make copies of maps, photographs, drawings, graphs, or other illustrations that you might want to add to make your report more interesting. Be certain to make a note of where you found the material for your bibliography.

Name: _____ Date: _____

Using the Internet

One advantage of using the Internet as a reference tool is that there is an enormous amount of material on nearly every topic.

The Internet can be especially helpful in writing about current event topics when you need the most up-to-date information.

If you have a computer at home, you can do much of your research there.

One disadvantage of the Internet is that it is not as well-organized as a library, and it can be difficult to find exactly what you need.

Another disadvantage is that anyone can have a website. Anyone can post articles on the Internet. That means that not all the information you find will be accurate. You must sometimes use your own good sense and judgment about the sources you use.

Websites that contain personal opinion essays may not be a good source for accurate information.

Look for websites sponsored by:

➢ colleges, schools, or educational publishers;

➢ government agencies like the Library of Congress;

➢ national organizations like the American Cancer Society;

➢ well-known companies; or

➢ television networks like the Discovery Channel or CNN news.

1. Would a website about hurricanes sponsored by The Weather Channel be a good source for information? Why or why not?

   _____

   _____

2. Would a report written by a sixth-grade student about why Abraham Lincoln is her favorite president be a good source for information? Why or why not?

   _____

   _____

3. Would a website sponsored by vegetarians be a good source for recipes for hamburger? Why or why not?

   _____

   _____

4. Why is it important to use good sense and judgment when searching the Internet?

   _____

   _____

   _____

Name: _____ Date: _____

Searching the Internet

➜ On the search engine page, type in a word or phrase to describe your topic, and click on GO or SEARCH.

➜ A list of websites related to your topic appears. The narrower the topic, the fewer choices will be available.

➜ If your topic is too broad, you may get thousands of possible websites!

➜ Try using different search words if you get too many choices, or too few.

Much like you narrowed your topic for your report, you may have to narrow your search. Just searching "The Civil War" will result in about 78,000,000 hits! What would be some better search terms?

_____

_____

1. Use the Internet to search for your topic. Which search engine did you use?

  _____

2. How many websites are listed for your topic? _____

3. Try another search engine or a different word. How many sites are available this time?

  _____

  _____

➜ Many websites might match the word you typed in, but not all of them will be what you want. You can get an idea of whether the site may be useful by reading the brief summary for each site.

➜ Click on the address of a site that looks like it might be helpful. If it's not what you want, click on the back button and try a different site.

4. Write the address of three sites that might be helpful for your report.

  _____

  _____

  _____

➜ When you find good websites, bookmark them or add them to your favorites list so you can find them again.

➜ Print articles that look useful. Then you can easily refer back to them when you aren't at the computer. You may also want to print pictures, graphs, maps, and other materials to include in your report.

Name: _____ Date: _____

Internet Cautions!

The Internet is a great tool, but there are some things to remember when using it:

A. **NEVER** give out your name, address, school location, or telephone number on the Internet without the consent of your parent or teacher.

B. **NEVER** send a picture of yourself over the Internet without the consent of your parent or teacher.

C. **NEVER** give out information about family members, friends, or classmates on the Internet.

D. **NEVER** provide information for other online activities like entering contests, newsletters, or clubs without permission.

E. **NEVER** click on pop-up ads or e-mails promising free stuff. These may infect your computer with viruses.

F. **NEVER** agree to get together with anyone you meet online without your parents' permission. People sometimes aren't who they say they are online.

G. If you see or receive something online that looks weird or bad or makes you feel uncomfortable, leave that site and tell your parents or teacher.

1. List two advantages of using the Internet as a reference tool.

   _____

   _____

   _____

   _____

   _____

   _____

2. List two disadvantages of using the Internet as a reference tool.

   _____

   _____

   _____

   _____

   _____

   _____

Name: _____   Date: _____

Other Sources

The library and Internet aren't the only sources of information you can use. Another option is to interview a **specialist** in that field. If you were writing a report on cattle, you might visit a ranch or talk to a veterinarian.

If you were writing a report on a type of plant, you could talk to someone who works in a nursery or visit a botanical garden.

Museums are good places to find information on a variety of topics. Many museums specialize in subjects like natural history, art, trains, sports, science, aviation, antique cars, or comic books. If you can't visit in person, many museums provide virtual tours online.

Historical societies and **historical sites** are good sources for information on local topics.

A **documentary** special on television or a video can be sources of information for your report.

For some topics, you might also do **firsthand observation**.

1. What type of person could you interview to learn more about your topic?

    _____

    _____

2. List three museums in your area. If you don't know of any, check the yellow pages in the telephone book or on the Internet.

    _____

    _____

    _____

3. What historical sites are in your area? If you don't know of any, check the yellow pages in the telephone book or on the Internet.

    _____

    _____

    _____

    _____

4. What other sources could you use, besides the library or the Internet, for your topic?

    _____

    _____

    _____

    _____

    _____

Name: _____ Date: _____

Taking Notes

★ Keep your questions in mind as you read articles and check other sources related to your topic. Write the answers you find on the pages where you wrote your questions.

★ It can be helpful to write the page number and the name of the book where you find material you plan to use, in case you want to go back to that source for more information later.

★ Your notes do not need to be written in complete sentences.

★ If you use any direct quotations, copy the material exactly as it is written, including spelling and punctuation. Write down who said it, when it was said, and where you found it. You'll need to cite this as a source in your bibliography.

★ Double-check any numbers you want to use to be certain you have them correct. It's easy to mix up a number, especially a large one.

★ Once you find enough answers, you can begin to organize your material.

★ If you have written questions and answers on separate sheets of paper, you can put the pages in an order that makes sense. This allows you to group material together and present it in a logical order.

★ Preparing an outline and creating a Venn diagram are two ways to help organize your material.

For each of your questions, write a one-sentence summary of the answers you found.

_____

_____

_____

_____

_____

_____

_____

_____

_____

Continue on your own paper if you need more room.

You can use these sentences to form the basis for each paragraph or section of your report.

Making an Outline to Organize

An **outline** is a helpful tool for organizing your thoughts and the material you've found for your report.

Follow the outline format shown for a report on the development of baseball. Your outline may vary, depending on the number of main points, related points, and examples.

[first main idea]	I. Early games similar to baseball
[a related idea]	A. Ancient Persian games
[another related idea]	B. Ancient Greek games
[another related idea]	C. Ancient Egyptian games
[another related idea]	D. Similar games in England
[an example]	1. cricket
[another example]	2. rounders
[another related idea]	E. Native American games
[second main idea]	II. First organized baseball clubs
	etc.

When preparing an outline, use words or short phrases, not complete sentences.

Make a rough outline for your topic.

1. On your own paper, use your notes to list your main ideas.

    Put them in the order in which you think you'll use them when you write your report. (It's all right if you change your mind later.)

    Number them I., II., III., IV., etc.

    Skip several lines between each main idea.

2. For each main idea, list two or more related ideas. Label them A., B., C., etc.

3. List examples for each related idea, if appropriate. Label them 1., 2., 3., etc.

4. Read through your rough outline.

    Check the order of your ideas. Make changes if needed.
    Check that you have included all the main points, related ideas, and examples. If you missed any, add them.

5. Rewrite your outline neatly.

Name: _____ Date: _____

Writing Your First Draft

When writing the first draft of your report, don't be overly concerned with spelling, grammar, and punctuation. Keep in mind that you'll need to correct any errors during the revision process.

A good report:

✔ Begins with an interesting topic sentence.

✔ Contains an opening paragraph that explains the scope of your report.

✔ Uses interesting words and sentences.

✔ Contains well-organized, interesting paragraphs with topic sentences for each new main idea.

✔ Presents material in a logical, sequential order.

✔ Is written in your own words and not copied from someone else's.

✔ Uses transitional sentences to lead from one paragraph to the next.

✔ Contains a conclusion paragraph that summarizes the main points of your research.

1. Write three possible sentences you might use to begin your report.

   _____

   _____

   _____

2. Write three possible sentences you might use in the concluding paragraph of your report.

   _____

   _____

   _____

3. On your own paper, write the first draft of your report.

Editing, Revising, and Proofreading Guide

When you edit and rewrite, you make corrections to your rough draft. You can change, add, and delete words or sentences as needed. Sometimes it helps to move sentences or paragraphs around so your report flows better. Writers often do several rough drafts before they are satisfied.

Use this guide to edit, revise, and proofread your report before you write the final copy.

Organization:

✔ Is your report clear and focused?

✔ Does your introductory paragraph clearly state the topic and scope of your report?

✔ Did you stick to your topic?

✔ Did you present the main points in the right order?

✔ Is your report organized in a logical way?

✔ Did you give specific examples?

✔ Did you leave out any important information?

✔ Did you include too much information?

✔ Does your conclusion sum up the information in your report?

✔ Did you include graphs, charts, illustrations, maps, or other types of visual material?

Grammar, Spelling, and Punctuation:

✔ Do all sentences begin with a capital letter?

✔ Do all sentences have end punctuation?

✔ Do all sentences have subjects and predicates?

✔ Do all subjects and predicates agree with each other?

✔ Are all words spelled correctly?

✔ Are all proper nouns capitalized?

✔ Do all of your sentences make sense?

When you are ready to write the final report, set it aside for a day. Then read it once more, to see if you need to make any changes or corrections.

The final report should be clean and error-free. It can be written by hand or typed on a computer, as specified by your teacher.

Most reports include a cover page with the title of your report, your name, and the date. The title of your report should provide a clue to what it's about. An interesting title encourages people to read your report.

Name: _____ Date: _____

Time to Review: Nonfiction

Use the words in the box to help you identify the statements related to nonfiction report-writing below. Write the correct term on the blank after each statement.

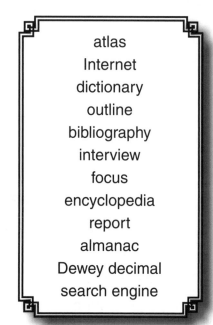

The word box contains:

atlas
Internet
dictionary
outline
bibliography
interview
focus
encyclopedia
report
almanac
Dewey decimal
search engine

1. A reference source that provides maps and information about countries, cities, population, time zones, mountains, bodies of water, etc.

    _____

2. A summary of information presented in a new, interesting way

    _____

3. A list of sources used to write a report

    _____

4. A reference source that provides articles in alphabetical order

    _____

5. A reference source that provides definitions of words _____

6. A reference source that can be used with a computer _____

7. Asking questions of a specialist in a field related to your topic

    _____

8. A reference source published yearly that contains statistics about sports, population, religion, national parks, movies, actors, and many other topics

    _____

9. The Internet software that helps you find information you are looking for

    _____

10. Numbering system used in libraries for nonfiction material _____

11. An organizational tool that summarizes the main points of a report _____

12. To go from a broad topic to a more specific one _____

Many Kinds of Reports

When writing a report, it is important to understand what kind of report your teacher wants you to write. There are five basic kinds of reports that your teacher might want you to write.

➤ Compare and Contrast: A compare and contrast report takes two things and examines how they are similar and how they are different. For example, a compare and contrast report on George Washington and Abraham Lincoln might examine how their presidencies were similar and different.

➤ Fact and Opinion: A fact and opinion report will examine which points of an argument are fact and which are opinion. For example, a report on circus animals might include facts such as where the animals came from and what they eat, as well as opinions some people have about circus animals, such as that they like performing or they should not be kept in cages.

➤ Persuasive Essay: A persuasive essay will try to convince your reader to make a change, such as accepting a new idea or taking a specific action. For example, a persuasive essay might try to convince the reader that your school should adopt new recycling rules. A persuasive essay will use facts to support your argument, such as how much paper could be recycled under the new rules compared with the current rules. Persuasive essays can also be in the form of movie or restaurant reviews.

➤ Cause and Effect: A cause and effect report focuses on an event, such as the Revolutionary War. A cause and effect report will then examine one of two questions. A cause question might be, What caused the Revolutionary War? The effect question might be, What happened as a result of the Revolutionary War? Sometimes, the teacher may want you to do both cause and effect in one report.

➤ Informational/How-To: Informational reports can cover topics such as when your town was founded or what happened at the City Council meeting on Monday. A how-to report provides step-by-step instructions on how to complete a task, such as using the new computer system at school.

When writing any of these reports, it is important to keep in mind all of the guidelines on spelling, capitalization, grammar, bibliographies, and organization of information. A good format helps your reader to understand your arguments instead of being distracted by sloppy work.

What Kind of Report?

Your teacher has given you an assignment to write a report. Match the kind of report to the title that best illustrates that report. You may use each choice more than once.

1. _____ Lower Speed Limits Save Lives

2. _____ Hurricane Ted: A City Recovers

3. _____ How To Paint Trees

4. _____ Everyone Should Learn Spanish

5. _____ Summer Break: An American Tradition

6. _____ Causes of the Great Depression

7. _____ The History of the Girl Scouts

8. _____ The American Buffalo

9. _____ The Disappearing Rain Forest: What We Should Do

10. _____ Mitosis: A Five Step Process

11. _____ Wilber and Babe the Pig: Talking Farm Animals

12. _____ The Meaning of "The Tell-Tale Heart"

13. _____ Careers in Math

14. _____ Pluto: Dwarf Planet

15. _____ Recycle—Or Else!

16. _____ The Deepest Lakes in the World

17. _____ Monet: Watercolor Genius

18. _____ What Happened After the Emancipation Proclamation

a. Persuasive Essay

b. Fact and Opinion

c. Compare and Contrast

d. Informational/ How-To

e. Cause and Effect

Name: _____ Date: _____

Compare and Contrast

Some reports **compare and contrast** two people, animals, objects, places, or ideas. You could write about the ways in which two sports, two planets, or two presidents are alike and the ways in which they are different.

1. For each topic, write another topic you could use in a comparison/contrast report.

   Abraham Lincoln _____

   The Grand Canyon _____

   Paris _____

   skunks _____

   spring _____

   bicycles _____

   A **Venn diagram** helps you organize ideas for a comparison/contrast report.

2. Fill in the Venn diagram with information comparing hockey and football, fruits and vegetables, or two items you will be comparing in your report. In the center where the circles overlap, write ideas about the ways in which the two items are alike.

   Write about the ways in which the two items are different in the parts of the diagram labeled Item 1 and Item 2.

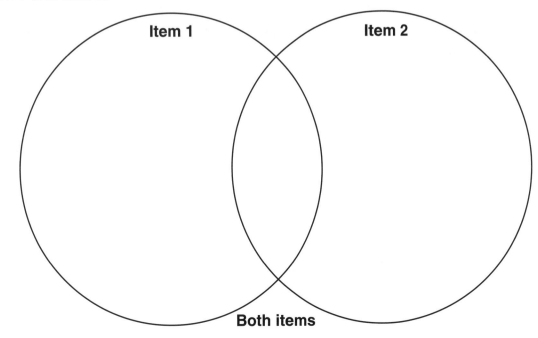

Advantages and Disadvantages

Advantage and disadvantage reports are a kind of compare and contrast report. In an advantage and disadvantage report, you are comparing and contrasting the positives (advantages) and negatives (disadvantages) of one or more things. You could write about the advantages and disadvantages of school uniforms (one thing), or you could write about the advantages and disadvantages of riding the bus or your bike to school (two things). In both reports, you would list the advantages of wearing uniforms or riding the bus as well as the disadvantages.

1. Choose one topic below and list the advantages and disadvantages.

    shorter school day   eliminating summer vacation

    getting a job or getting an allowance   being the oldest or youngest child

    buying bread or making your own   presidents and kings

    living in the city or living in a small town required math classes

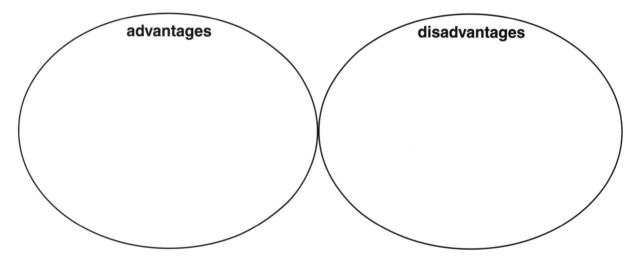

2. In the space below, write a great introduction that grabs your reader's interest about your topic.

    _____

    _____

    _____

    _____

    _____

    _____

    _____

    _____

    _____

3. Continue your essay on your own paper.

Name: _____ Date: _____

Facts and Opinions

Facts can be proven through direct observation or by checking a reliable reference source.

As you search for information for your report, you may find "facts" that don't agree. How do you know which source to believe? If sources list different numbers for the population of a city, you should use the most current source. Also consider the source. Population numbers from the U.S. Census Bureau would be more reliable than numbers from an un-cited blog.

Sometimes, sources list different dates for an event that happened long ago. That may be because written records were not kept at that time. It could also mean that new evidence or records have been discovered.

If you find two sources that disagree on a fact, check a third source. Which of the sources seems more reliable? Which is the most current?

Use common sense and good judgment, especially when using Internet sources. Ask yourself: Who wrote this? What makes this person an expert? Is the person presenting facts or opinions?

Opinions express someone's view or belief.

> **Fact:** Phoenix is a city in Arizona.
> You can prove it by looking in any U.S. atlas.
> You can go there and check for yourself.

> **Opinion:** Phoenix is the best city in Arizona.
> This cannot be proven. Even if you went to every city in Arizona and decided for yourself that Phoenix was the best city, it would still be an opinion.

Read the statement. Write "F" for fact or "O" for opinion.

_____ 1. Alaska is the largest state in the U.S.

_____ 2. Miami is east of St. Louis.

_____ 3. Living in Maine is better than living in California.

_____ 4. Chicago is nicknamed the Windy City.

_____ 5. Rainy days are depressing.

_____ 6. The average annual rainfall is higher in Wisconsin than in Nevada.

Name: _____ Date: _____

How Large Is the Amazon River?

Facts are statements that are true. They can be proven by checking reliable sources or through direct observation. Facts are important when writing news articles, reports, and informational essays.

Fact: The Amazon River is the largest river system on Earth.

You could prove this by measuring the volume of water in all the rivers on Earth for yourself, but that would be a lot of work.

1. How else could you check to find out if this statement is a fact?

   _____

   _____

Opinions are statements that express someone's point of view. In advertisements, editorials, letters, stories, and most types of essays, writers include both facts and opinions.

Opinion: The Mississippi River is the prettiest river in the United States.

2. Even if you took a trip on every river in the United States and decided for yourself that the Mississippi River was the prettiest, would that make it a fact, rather than an opinion?

   _____

For each statement, write "F" for Fact or "O" for Opinion. For each fact, list one way you could verify it. If the statement is an opinion, leave the line blank.

3. _____ Everybody enjoys a circus.

   _____

4. _____ More people have dogs than cats as pets.

   _____

5. _____ Michigan is farther north than Missouri.

   _____

6. _____ Fly-Me Airlines offers the most convenient schedules.

   _____

7. Write a fact: _____

8. Write an opinion: _____

Persuasive Reports: What's Your Opinion?

Opinion papers, also called persuasive reports, are designed to persuade the reader to agree with the author's opinion. To write a persuasive report, select a topic about which you feel strongly. You won't be able to write very well if you really don't care one way or another.

Your report can agree or disagree with an issue. It can be for or against a candidate or proposal. Your report can discuss a problem and offer solutions that might help solve the problem.

Select one of these topics for a persuasive report:

A. All students, beginning in fourth grade, should or should not be required to take a foreign language every year until they graduate from high school.

B. Your school should or should not have a dress code that does not allow jeans, shorts, T-shirts, or sweatshirts at school.

C. All windows in classrooms should or should not be completely covered, because looking outside is a distraction to students.

D. Summer vacations should or should not be only one month long, and the school year should last 11 months.

E. The school cafeteria should or should not only offer vegetarian meals: no meat—only fruits, vegetables, and fish.

F. A person who had been convicted of a crime and spent two years in jail for robbery 20 years ago should or should not be elected mayor of your city.

G. The legal age for obtaining a driver's license should or should not be raised to 21.

1. On your own paper, write a letter to the editor of the local newspaper, expressing your opinion about one of the topics.

2. Remember to:

   • State the issue and how you feel about it.

   • Give specific reasons or examples for your opinion.

   • Add a one-sentence summary.

3. Edit, revise, and proofread your editorial before rewriting it.

Name: _____ Date: _____

Convince Me

To **persuade** means to convince someone to make a change, such as accepting a new idea, taking a specific action, voting for a candidate, or considering a different point of view.

A persuasive essay includes:

- A clear statement of the writer's position.
  Example: Recycling is important.

- Several reasons or examples to support that point of view.
  Example: Recycling saves land resources.
  Recycling reduces pollution.
  Recycling preserves wildlife habitats.

- Reasons why this would be beneficial to the individual reader.
  Example: If everyone recycles, the earth will be a better place in which to live.

Writers use different methods or a combination of methods to persuade readers.

- Comparison and contrast:
  My way is better because ...

- Flattery/guilt:
  If you are a good person, you will do what I suggest.

- Experts/statistics:
  Scientists have discovered ....
  Nine out of ten people agree ....

- Everyone is doing it:
  And you should too.

1. How is a persuasion essay like an advertisement?

   _____

   _____

   _____

2. If you were going to write a persuasive essay to convince readers to vote for you for mayor, which method do you think would work best?

   _____

   _____

3. Write an example of how you could use one of these methods in your essay.

   _____

   _____

   _____

Name: _____ Date: _____

Time for a Change

1. Use the graphic organizer to gather ideas for a persuasive essay. You can write about one of these topics, or use your own ideas:

   - Become a vegetarian.
   - Wear your seat belt.
   - Get more exercise.
   - Donate blood.
   - Wear a biking helmet.
   - Vote for me.
   - Take a vacation to the North Pole.

Statement of your position:

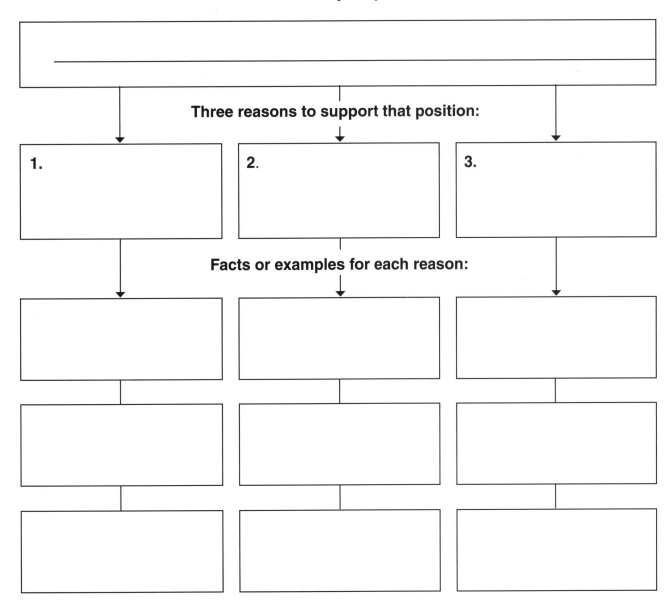

Three reasons to support that position:

1.

2.

3.

Facts or examples for each reason:

2. On your own paper, write a persuasive essay to convince readers to make a change. Include specific reasons why the reader should make that change and how it would benefit the reader.

Name: _____ Date: _____

A Persuasive Letter

Have you ever tried to talk your parents into letting you do something, buy something, or go someplace?

1. Describe a time when you tried, but failed.

   _____

   _____

   _____

Have you ever tried to persuade a friend or relative to make a change, get rid of a bad habit, or try harder?

2. Did you succeed? Why or why not? _____

   _____

   _____

Have you ever asked for a favor, a special privilege, or a chance to try out for a sports team?

3. Describe what happened. _____

   _____

   _____

Most people encounter these types of situations quite frequently. Instead of talking to convince someone to accept your point of view, you could write a persuasive letter.

The advantages of writing a persuasive letter are:

- You can state your position clearly.

- You can use facts, examples, or statistics to support your position.

- You can predict arguments against your position and answer them in your letter.

- You can take your time and plan your words carefully.

4. On your own paper, write a persuasive letter. You can use one of these suggestions or any idea of your own.

   - request a larger allowance
   - get permission to adopt a pet
   - ask for a special privilege
   - convince someone to stop smoking

   - change a school rule
   - try out for a team
   - get picked to attend a special event
   - present a vacation idea

Looking at Both Sides

People naturally seem to disagree on things. Is chocolate your favorite flavor? Some people prefer vanilla. Is blue your favorite color? Many people prefer red—or green—or purple. If people can't even agree on the best flavor or their favorite color, how can they ever agree on really important things?

Considering both sides of an issue, looking at it from different points of view, and trying to be objective may not cause you to change your mind, but it will allow you to understand the other person's point of view better.

What if your school board proposed changing the school calendar so that students attend school year-round? Instead of having three months off in the summer, they would have one week off every month.

Before you express your opinion, think about the idea for a while. Work with a partner to come up with reasons for and against this proposal. Consider how this change would affect different people and how they may feel about it.

Students would like this proposal because: _____

_____

_____

_____

_____

_____

_____

Students would not like this proposal because: _____

_____

_____

_____

_____

_____

_____

Continue on the next page.

Name: _____ Date: _____

Looking at Both Sides (cont.)

Proposal: Change the school calendar so that students attend school all year, with one week off every month.

Parents would like this proposal because: _____
_____
_____

Parents would not like this proposal because: _____
_____
_____

Teachers would like this proposal because: _____
_____
_____

Teachers would not like this proposal because: _____
_____
_____

Other reasons why this proposal would be a good idea: _____
_____
_____
_____

Other reasons why this proposal would not be a good idea: _____
_____
_____
_____

After considering as many points of view as possible, what is your opinion? ____
_____
_____
_____

Write a journal entry that looks at both sides of an issue.

Name: _____ Date: _____

Reviews: Dine at Tom's Tuna Towne

Reviews ...

• Describe books, movies, software, plays, CDs, websites, and other products.

• Can also describe places, like a restaurant, museum, or new park.

• Combine experience and opinion. A writer can't review a book without reading it or give an opinion of a restaurant without eating there.

• Include what the author liked and disliked about the product or place and why the reader should or should not buy it, read it, watch it, visit it, etc.

For each statement, write "F" for Fact or "O" for Opinion.

1. _____ The tuna surprise was the best item on the menu at Tom's Tuna Towne restaurant.

2. _____ The new park has the largest circular slide in the state.

3. _____ The movie, "Ha!" starred Vincent Price and Boris Karloff.

4. _____ "Ha!" was a really funny movie.

5. _____ "Ha!" is the best movie ever made.

6. _____ Tom's Tuna Towne featured seven different types of tuna casserole.

7. _____ The Pottery Channel website included many links to other pottery sites.

8. _____ You should read *Don't Look Behind You* if you like mysteries.

9. _____ The new CD by the Magic Triangles is their best so far.

10. _____ None of the songs on the new Magic Triangles CD have ever been recorded before.

Firsthand Experience

Name something specific you could write about for each type of review below, such as the title of a book you've read, a restaurant where you've eaten, or a movie you've watched. Remember, you need **firsthand experience** to write a review.

1. A book: _____

2. A movie: _____

3. Computer software: _____

4. A website: _____

5. A music CD: _____

6. A restaurant: _____

7. A television program: _____

8. A theme park: _____

9. A new store: _____

10. A museum: _____

11. A specific brand of food: _____

12. Your favorite vegetable: _____

13. A clothing fashion: _____

14. A television commercial: _____

_____

15. Select any of the above items for a review. Include reasons for what you like and what you don't like about the item and your recommendation for the reader.

16. Write your review on your own paper. Edit, revise, and proofread before you rewrite.

Name: _____ Date: _____

Informational Reports: Answering Six Questions

Informational reports are one of the most common writing assignments. Informational reports do exactly what they say—they provide information to the reader about a topic. Informational reports should focus on facts; opinions do not belong in an informational report. In an informational report, you need to answer six questions about your topic: Who, What, When, Where, Why, and How. For example, imagine you have been assigned a three-page report on the Declaration of Independence. Your answers to the six questions might look like this:

- ➤ Who: Thomas Jefferson, John Adams, Ben Franklin, and others
- ➤ What: A document declaring independence from England
- ➤ When: 1776
- ➤ Where: Philadelphia
- ➤ Why: To establish the reasons why America was declaring independence
- ➤ How: Colonies sent representatives to Philadelpia to the Second Continental Congress

After you identify your answers to these six questions, then you can begin to build your report in a way that informs readers what happened in a clear, easy-to-understand way.

1. Choose a topic from below.

The Emancipation Proclamation	Mt. St. Helens
The Great Wall of China	the student council election
Columbus discovers the New World	polar bears
Easter Island	Edgar Allen Poe's "The Raven"

2. In the spaces below, answer the six questions about your topic.

    Who? _____

    What? _____

    When? _____

    Where? _____

    Why? _____

    How? _____

3. Write an opening sentence about your topic.

    _____

4. What would you call this report? Come up with a title that encourages your reader to keep reading.

    _____

Name: _____   Date: _____

Informational Reports: Answering Six Questions (cont.)

Choose a topic of your own and prewrite for your informational report by answering the six questions about your topic below.

1. Your topic: _____

2. Who (or what) was involved? _____

    _____

    _____

3. What happened? _____

    _____

    _____

4. When did it happen? _____

    _____

    _____

5. Where did it happen? _____

    _____

    _____

6. Why did it happen? _____

    _____

    _____

7. How did it happen? _____

    _____

    _____

8. What happened as a result? _____

    _____

    _____

9. What would be a good title for this report?

    _____

Name: _____ Date: _____

Editing an Informational Report

Informational reports should focus on facts; opinions do not belong in an informational report. Edit the first paragraphs of an informational report on economics below. Cross out any sentence that does not belong in an informational report. Then read the paragraphs again to check for spelling and grammatical errors. Rewrite the corrected paragraph on your own paper.

Economics

Economics is the study of how things are bought and sold. When You go to the the store and buy milk, you is participating in the local economy. This is the best kind of economy. When your parents buy a new house, they are participating in the national economy. This kind of economy is good, too. And when you buy something made in China like a microwave, you are participating in the Global economy. The Global economy isn't all bad, but it's beter to do the local economy. To be a part of an economy, you must uby and sell goods or services.

Goods and services are teh products that satisify our needs and wants. goods are any items that can be bought and sold Some examples of goods are clothing bicycles, breakfast cereals, and computers. A service, is any action that one person or group does for another for money. some people who provide services include teachers, cooks, lawyers, bankers, hair stylists, and nurses. Its better to spend more money on services to get better service. You don't want no bad service.

Name: _____ Date: _____

How-To Reports: First, Get a Really Large Toothbrush ...

One kind of informational report is a **how-to report**. A how-to report informs the reader about what steps to take in order to complete a task or learn something new. To write **how-to instructions** for performing a task, you should include a specific list of the materials and tools needed and an explanation of how to use them (if necessary).

Steps should be listed in order. Each step in the process should be clearly explained. Use your own paper if you need more room.

1. To write instructions for cutting out paper snowflakes, what information should you include?

   _____

   _____

   _____

   _____

2. To explain how to play a computer game, what types of information would you need to include?

   _____

   _____

   _____

   _____

3. To brush a hippo's teeth, what types of information should you include?

   _____

   _____

   _____

   _____

   _____

   _____

4. On your own paper, write clear, step-by-step in-structions for washing a car, giving a dog a bath, building a pair of stilts, or hitting a home run.

5. Include any diagrams or illustrations needed to clarify the instructions.

6. When you finish writing, read through your instructions.

   • Did you list all the materials needed?   • Did you miss any steps?
   • Did you write the steps in order?   • Are all the directions clear?

7. Edit, revise, proofread, and rewrite the instructions.

Name: _____ Date: _____

Cause and Effect Reports

Every event has causes and effects. Cause and effect reports begin with a specific event, such as the Civil War or Jackie Robinson breaking the color barrier in baseball. Sometimes, the teacher will want you to examine only the causes of that event. For example, what caused the Civil War? If you were writing this paper, you might want to talk about the following causes:

➢ Slavery
➢ Different opinions on how much control the federal government should have
➢ Whether or not new states should be free states or slave states
➢ Taxes on goods sold across state lines

All of these reasons helped contribute to the Civil War.

Other times, your teacher might want you to examine the effects of an event. For example, if your topic was Jackie Robinson breaking the color barrier in Major League Baseball, you might want to talk about the following effects:

➢ Integrated Major League Baseball
➢ Helped kick-start the Civil Rights movement
➢ Demanded respect as human beings for African Americans
➢ First on-air African-American sports announcer

Occasionally, your teacher might want you to look at the causes and effects of an event. For example, Francis Scott Key wrote "The Star-Spangled Banner." The cause of this event was Key being held prisoner on a British ship during a nighttime battle. The effect was a patriotic poem that was adopted as our national anthem.

Match the causes and the effects below.

Causes

1. _____ Charles Dickens wrote *A Christmas Carol*.

2. _____ Sir Issac Newton was hit by a falling apple.

3. _____ Alexander the Great conquered Persia.

4. _____ Gold was discovered in California.

5. _____ Earth is tilted at a 23.5° angle.

6. _____ The stock market crashed in 1929.

7. _____ Henry Ford built cars on an assembly line.

8. _____ Alaska became the 49th state.

Effects

a. We have four seasons.
b. Greek culture became widespread.
c. The Great Depression lasted more than a decade.
d. He discovered the Laws of Gravity.
e. Cars became affordable and most people got one.
f. It became one of the best-loved holiday stories of all time.
g. It became the largest state.
h. The Gold Rush led millions of people to go west.

Cause and Effect: The Clock Struck Midnight

Cause: The clock struck midnight.
Effect: Cinderella's coach turned back into a pumpkin.

For each **cause**, write a possible **effect**. Use complete sentences.

Cause	*Effect*

1. A hurricane hit the east coast of Florida. _____

    _____

    _____

2. Maysie didn't study for her history test. _____

    _____

    _____

3. Sam finished his report two days before it was due. _____

    _____

    _____

4. Millions of people read about the adventures of Harry Potter. _____

    _____

    _____

For each **effect**, write a possible **cause**. Use complete sentences.

5. _____ They spent the day shoveling snow.

    _____

    _____

6. _____ None of the athletes received gold medals.

    _____

    _____

7. _____ The terrified dog finally stopped shaking.

    _____

    _____

8. _____ By the time they arrived at the park, everyone was very hungry.

    _____

    _____

Name: _____ Date: _____

Time To Review: Types of Reports

Use the words in the box to complete this activity. Place the correct term on the blank after each statement.

> compare and contrast
> facts
> opinions
> persuade
> cause
> effect
> informational report
> review
> how-to report
> advantages
> disadvantages
> firsthand

1. An event that leads to another event happening

   _____

2. The positives or upside

   _____

3. To convince the reader to agree with the author's

   opinion _____

4. A report that examines the ways two things are similar

   and different _____

5. Statements that can be proven through direct observation

   or reliable sources _____

6. Statements that reflect what someone believes _____

7. Written to provide information about events or people

   _____

8. A combination of facts and opinions by a writer about a place, book, movie, etc.

   _____

9. Writing that explains clearly how to do something

   _____

10. The negatives or downside _____

11. The results of something that happened _____

12. Something you personally saw, did, or read _____

Answer Keys

Note: Answers in most of the writing exercises will vary. Only exercises with definite answers are listed below.

Personal Writing

Electronic Media (page 12)
1. T   2. F   3. F   4. T
5. F   6. F   7. T   8. T

Time to Review: Personal Writing (page 13)
1. goals
2. anecdote
3. emotions
4. business letter
5. journaling
6. blog
7. friendly letter
8. electronic media
9. e-mail
10. snail mail
11. autobiography
12. bloggers

Descriptive Writing

To Capitalize or Not to Capitalize? (page 19)

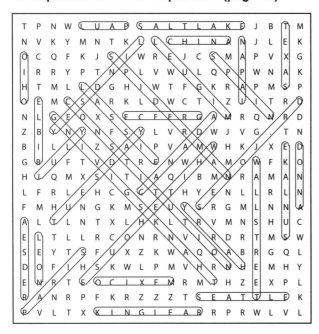

Synonyms (page 29)
Answers will vary, but may include:
1. jog, sprint
2. witnessed, viewed
3. listened, eavesdropped
4. hilarious, amusing
5. weird, odd
6. pleasant, friendly
7. calm, gentle
8. deafening, noisy
9. thrilling, exhilarating
10. Paragraphs will vary.

Finish the Pictures (page 30)
Manticore:

All other pictures will vary.

Active Voice, Active Writing (page 35)
1. A   2. P   3. P   4. A
5. P   6. A   7. A   8. A
9. Sentences will vary.

A Streak of Lightning (page 38)
1. mood, thunderstorm
2. trip, nightmare
3. mall, zoo
4. fog, cat
5. eagle, streak of lightning
All other answers will vary.

Like Walking on Eggs (page 40)
1. red tape: paperwork; bureaucracy
2. rained cats and dogs: rained very hard
3. rolled out the red carpet: made someone feel very welcome or royal
4. bundle of nerves: worried or upset
5. butterflies in his stomach: nervous or scared
6. down in the dumps: depressed or sad
7. button your lip: keep silent
8. blew her stack: got very upset or angry

Time to Review: Descriptive Writing (page 42)
1. similes
2. idioms
3. adjectives
4. metaphors
5. synonyms
6. conclusion
7. sensory words
8. thesaurus
9. paragraph
10. antonyms
11. supporting sentences
12. topic sentence

Fiction

Punctuating Dialogue (page 51)
1. "Christmas won't be Christmas without any presents,"
2. "It's so dreadful to be poor!"
3. "I don't think it's fair for some girls to have lots of pretty things, and other girls nothing at all,"
4. "We've got Father and Mother and each other,"
5. "We haven't got Father, and shall not have him for a long time."
6. "You know the reason Mother proposed not having any presents this Christmas was because it's going to be a hard winter for everyone, and she thinks we ought not to spend money for pleasures when our men are suffering so in the army."

Writing and Punctuating Dialogue (page 52)
1. "What 'cha doing, Tom?" asked Henry as he shuffled his bare feet in the dirt.
2. Tom studied the fence before answering, "Well, you see, Henry, I'm creating a work of art."
3. "Looks to me like you're painting a fence, Tom," (Answers will vary) Henry.
4. "No," (Answers will vary) Tom. "Painting a fence would be work and everyone knows how I feel about work."
5. "Is painting a fence a game? Can I play?" Henry (Answers will vary) eagerly.
6. "Oh no!" (Answers will vary) Tom with a wink at his brother.
7. "I'll give you my dead toad if you let me paint a while," (Answers will vary) Henry. "Please."
8. Tom thought a while, then shook his head. "I reckon Aunt Polly wouldn't allow it. She's mighty particular."

Time to Review: Fiction (page 64)
1. tall tales
2. mysteries
3. fantasies
4. setting
5. antagonist
6. fables
7. myths
8. thesaurus
9. dialogue
10. plot
11. science fiction

Poetry

Punctuating Poetry (pages 70–71)
I went to the animal fair.
The lions and tigers were there.
An old baboon
By the light of the moon
Was combing his long red hair.

A monkey got in a funk.
He tripped on the elephant's trunk.
The elephant sneezed
And fell to his knees.
Well, that was the end of the monk.

Thunderstorm
Bolts of lightning
Ripping apart the sky,
Shattering the night,
Flashing off and on
Like a demented strobe light.

Lost and Found
Where do thoughts go when you lose them?
Do they vanish forever?
If you find a lost thought,
Can you pretend it followed you home
And claim it for your own?

A Rainbow Garden
Red, blue, purple, orange, and yellow flowers
Shout to passersby with their brightly colored blooms.
Her garden was a rainbow of
Tulips, roses, daisies, and lilies,
Free for all to enjoy.

Writing Haiku (page 75)
1. 5, 7, 5

Nonsense Poems: Limericks (page 79)
1. Lines one, two, and five: *lad*, *bad*, *dad*
   Lines three and four: *worse* and *verse*
2. Line one: 9
   Line two: 9
   Line three: 5
   Line four: 5
   Line five: 9

Time to Review: Poetry (page 82)
1. metaphors
2. sensory poems
3. Robert Frost
4. couplet
5. limericks
6. alliteration
7. poetry
8. haiku
9. narrative poem
10. descriptive poetry
11. thesaurus
12. repetition

Nonfiction

Finding Material at the Library (page 91)
2. 551.7 is a lower number than 551.71
3. Although the numbers are the same, L comes before M in the alphabet, so that book would come first.
4. A. 2   B. 5   C. 8   D. 6   E. 7
   F. 3   G. 10   H. 1   I. 9   J. 4

Using the Internet (page 94)
1. Yes. It is a well-respected television network that specializes in weather, and it employs meteorologists and other scientists.
2. No. It is an opinion essay, and the sixth-grader got her information from other souces, so it probably has no direct information.
3. No. Vegetarians don't eat hamburger, so they probably wouldn't know how to develop and cook a good-tasting hamburger recipe.
4. Anyone can post information on the Internet, so not all of it is accurate. You have to evaluate which sources are reliable.

Time to Review: Nonfiction (page 102)
1. atlas
2. report
3. bibliography
4. encyclopedia
5. dictionary
6. Internet
7. interview
8. almanac
9. search engine
10. Dewey decimal
11. outline
12. focus

Types of Reports

What Kind of Report? (page 104)
1. b
2. e
3. d
4. a
5. d
6. e
7. d
8. d
9. a
10. d
11. c
12. b
13. d
14. d
15. a
16. d
17. b
18. e

Facts and Opinions (page 107)
1. F
2. F
3. O
4. F
5. O
6. F

How Large Is the Amazon River? (page 108)
1. Answers will vary.
2. opinion
3. O
4. F
5. F
6. O
Ways to verify facts will vary.

Reviews: Dine at Tom's Tuna Towne (page 115)
1. O
2. F
3. F
4. O
5. O
6. F
7. F
8. O
9. O
10. F

Editing an Informational Report (page 119)
Corrected paragraphs:

Economics is the study of how things are bought and sold. When you go to the store and buy milk, you are participating in the local economy. When your parents buy a new house, they are participating in the national economy. And when you buy something made in China, you are participating in the global economy. To be a part of an economy, you must buy and sell goods or services.

Goods and services are the products that satisfy our needs and wants. Goods are any items that can be bought or sold. Some examples of goods are clothing, bicycles, breakfast cereals, and computers. A service is any action that one person or group does for another for money. Some people who provide services include teachers, cooks, lawyers, bankers, hair stylists, and nurses.

Cause and Effect Reports (page 121)
1. f
2. d
3. b
4. h
5. a
6. c
7. e
8. g

Time to Review: Types of Reports (page 123)
1. cause
2. advantages
3. persuade
4. compare and contrast
5. facts
6. opinions
7. informational report
8. review
9. how-to report
10. disadvantages
11. effect
12. firsthand